The Constitution of The United Peoples of Earth

Abhijit Naskar is the twenty-first century mind of science, whose gentle and glorious philosophical touch has enabled modern Neuroscience to effectively engage in the human society towards diminishing the ever-growing conflicts among religions. As an untiring advocate of global harmony and peace, he became a beloved best-selling author all over the world with his very first book "The Art of Neuroscience in Everything". With various of his pioneering ventures into the Neuropsychology of religious sentiments, he has hugely contributed in the eradication of religious differences in our world, for which he is popularly hailed as a humanitarian neuroscientist, who takes the human civilization in the path of sweet general harmony.

THE
CONSTITUTION
OF THE
UNITED PEOPLES
OF EARTH

ABHIJIT NASKAR

Also by Abhijit Naskar

The Art of Neuroscience in Everything
Your Own Neuron: A Tour of Your Psychic Brain
The God Parasite: Revelation of Neuroscience
The Spirituality Engine
Love Sutra: The Neuroscientific Manual of Love
Homo: A Brief History of Consciousness
Neurosutra: The Abhijit Naskar Collection
Autobiography of God: Biopsy of A Cognitive Reality
Biopsy of Religions: Neuroanalysis towards Universal
Tolerance
Prescription: Treating India's Soul
What is Mind?
In Search of Divinity: Journey to The Kingdom of Conscience
Love, God & Neurons: Memoir of a scientist who found
himself by getting lost
The Islamophobic Civilization: Voyage of Acceptance
Neurons of Jesus: Mind of A Teacher, Spouse & Thinker
Neurons, Oxygen & Nanak
The Education Decree
Principia Humanitas
The Krishna Cancer
Rowdy Buddha: The First Sapiens
We Are All Black: A Treatise on Racism
The Bengal Tigress: A Treatise on Gender Equality
Either Civilized or Phobic: A Treatise on Homosexuality
Wise Mating: A Treatise on Monogamy
Illusion of Religion: A Treatise on Religious
Fundamentalism
The Film Testament
Human Making is Our Mission: A Treatise on Parenting
I Am The Thread: My Mission
7 Billion Gods: Humans Above All
Lord is My Sheep: Gospel of Human
Morality Absolute
A Push in Perception
Let The Poor Be Your God
Conscience over Nonsense
Saint of The Sapiens
Time to Save Medicine
Fabric of Humanity
Build Bridges not Walls: In the name of Americana

DEDICATION

For My Family of 7 Billion

CONTENTS

Introduction to A Better World

Mainspring of Life (A Sonnet)

I have no nationality except humanity,

I have no tradition except compassion,

I have no religion except liberty,

I have no god except a family of 7 billion,

I have no belief but only awareness,

I have no creed but only acceptance,

I have no messiah except the self,

I have no scripture except my conscience,

I have no gospel except godliness,

I have no sermon except thought,

I have no philosophy except oneness,

I have nothing to give you except love a whole
lot,

I demand no obedience, nor do I desire worship
and offering,

For there is death in worship, and freedom is
life's mainspring.

A better world begins with a better human. Are you a better human! Don't answer me - think over the question in your mind. Ask yourself the question, over and over again, till all the mist covering the answer disappears. The more you ask the question, the more it'll become clear that, a better human is simply a human not bound by labels of culture, religion, race or anything else. How can the world be a better place, when the humans in it are not ready to budge the slightest bit from their rugged culturally ordained lifestyle and perception of life!

Life began from a single cell - from that single cell an entire kingdom of animals was born, and we the humans happen to be only one among those 8.7 million species. Earlier in our life as a species, we were living in the wild savanna of Africa, alongside our fellow animals. But we have come a long way since then, and this long way has been led mostly by the misfits, by those who are deemed by their society as abnormal.

Progress and normality can never go hand in hand - progress and security can never go hand in hand - you must let go of one to have the other. But the unfortunate reality of this world is, most humans are not psychologically capable enough to do so - to let go of security - that's why they cannot lead in the path of progress, since it is filled with insecurity. Hence rises the need for misfits or anomalies.

Progress requires sacrifice of security. And the only reason, humanity keeps on progressing, despite the fact that most of the human population do not sacrifice their security, is that, on behalf of the whole humanity, a handful of bravehearts do all the sacrificing and pain-bearing, yet people can't manage to comprehend that we couldn't have become the masters of this planet by living a comfortable and secure life. To have great progress, one must sacrifice small pleasures.

The masses have a safe and secure existence not because of their actions, but because of those handful of lionhearts, who go beyond personal gain to make a species move ahead, despite being mocked and laughed at every step of the way, by the very people, for whom they sacrifice all. The sun doesn't ask for admiration in return for its light and warmth. And this may sound glorious and encouraging, but remember, once you choose to walk on the path of service, each footstep would feel like you are stepping on burning charcoals.

So, here comes the difference between a philosophical notion and its actual practical implications. It's one thing to read or talk about serving humanity beyond personal gain and another to actually walk on that path for life. The path of service is but a thorn-infested trail in the woods - a trail that is not yet made a trail, but simply lies indistinguishable from the rest of the jungle. And the work of a torch-bearer of progress is to make the trail appear and soften the thorns by crushing them with their own footsteps, while bearing an infinite amount of agony.

Agony is a fundamental companion in progress - we bear agony, so that the masses don't have to. It's the prerogative of the masses to live in comfort and security, but those who want to pull the cart of progress ahead, can't have that luxury. The day the sun starts asking reward for the light and warmth it gives to the world, would be the last day of the sun's existence. So, be the sun and keep shining over the world, regardless of whether you are admired or not.

I keep working in solitude and agony with no one by my side, day after day, without any hope for personal happiness, for I carry the responsibility to unify the humans, by pointing out to them, with evidence, their innate oneness beyond all sectarianism - and I do so, not out of any sort of compulsion, rather, because that's who I am - I am no human - I am the unifying force of nature - I am the One and I am the All - in me lies the possibility of human harmony - in me lies the possibility of human acceptance - I am the driving force of conscience - I am the absolute timeless ocean of unified sentience.

Preamble

There are two kinds of people in the world - first those who run away from danger, then there are those who run towards danger, to see if someone needs help. And today's world, I'm pain-stricken say, is filled mostly with the first kind of people. Everybody only cares for themselves and their immediate family, and the problems of even the next-door neighbor are of no concern to them, because that's not their family, hence they feel that that's not their responsibility. But the time has finally arisen, that we make it our business to be concerned of the people that surround us, regardless of whether they are directly related to us or not.

Strangers must be made family, for in assimilation lies salvation for humanity. So, rise, my thinking sibling, wherever you are right now, and take the eternal pledge with me - "**I, a living, breathing and above all, conscientious creature of planet earth, do solemnly swear to none but myself, that no matter the circumstances, I shall always stand by the people of my kind, my humanity, beyond the bounds of race, religion, gender, tradition and**

sexual orientation - I shall accept differences, but not differentiation - I shall accept both belief and disbelief, but not discrimination - I shall accept both intellect and ignorance, but not arrogance - I shall observe the good and bad from all backgrounds, and accept only the good while discarding the vices and violence."

And this is no altruism, rather, it's just plain and pure human existence, for the best kind of existence is to exist for others, as much as you exist for yourself and your immediate family. Say to yourself, if humanity is in misery, it may not be my fault, but if I die leaving humanity with the same amount of misery, then it is my fault.

When I was a kid, my father stuck a little note on my reading lamp, that said "stop not till you reach your goal". At that time, I believe he wanted me to be successful in life, but what he could not comprehend, was that my goal was not like that of the most of the population. My goal – my purpose – the reason for my existence is only one – it is to ensure that humanity doesn't lose sight of its humanity, in the constant battle between beliefs – between ideologies – between opinions – between religious orthodoxy and radical reasoning.

Fight, fight and fight – all they do is fight – they don't care about harmony or world peace, all they care about is to prove that they are right and others are wrong – the scientists, the philosophers, the preachers, the spiritualists – every single one of them (excluding the exceptions) just want to triumph over the other – and that's precisely what's wrong with this world – they all want victory to be their exclusive possession and defeat to be the possession of the others. This way, no amount of riches will ever bring happiness and harmony in this world, because to have happiness and harmony, we all must act together to rise triumphant as one species, and not as individuals or tiny groups.

From an insignificant bunch of apes in a corner of Africa we have become the masters of an entire planet – and still if we can't have the sense of unity, then what's the use of all this power and all the glorious intellect of which we are so proud of! Throw away such intellect that doesn't bring people together – throw away such scriptures that create walls rather than bridges – throw away such institutions that proclaim exclusive authority over divinity – throw away such reasoning that barres you from accepting human weakness. Throw away every single trace of inhumanity, regardless of their intellectual or non-intellectual grounds. Intellect without humanity, is as dangerous as religious fundamentalism.

Similar to religious fundamentalism, unrestrained intellect can make a person blind to the psychological necessities of others, for physical necessities are much easier to notice than those of the psyche. That's why many sophisticated atheist intellectuals find it rather civilized and glorious to talk most boastfully about the harms of religion in the human society, while being completely unaware of the society's psychological reliance over religion and even when a few of them are aware of it, they somehow fail to realize in their bones, the existential significance of it all, because they talk with the force of intellect and not with the whole force of life. And that's where the necessity of metaphysics comes in, for metaphysics is simply the realization of reality as it is, and not as how we believe it to be. And this belief beyond reality is prevalent, both on the side of religious fundamentalism and militant atheism or atheistic fundamentalism, for they both deny basic human necessity, if it doesn't suit their own perception.

There is no Lord Almighty up there with a divine concern for life on a tiny blue planet – that's a fact, but if we put all our focus on this fact only, then we shall never ever be able to diminish the differences between people. In the pursuit of proving one side to be right, humanity keeps on losing all together. So, the focus must shift – it must shift from argumentation to the solution of real problems of this planet.

And we cannot do that, unless we first put aside our primal desire for petty victory as individuals or tiny groups. Remember, wise is not the one who wins always, but the one who knows where to lose. So, it's time that we start thinking about collective victory over personal victory. And in fact, those who truly desire to make this world a better place for future generations, would never see collective victory to be separate from personal victory – so, if you are such a person, you would see your own victory in the victory of humanity – in the victory of others.

Rise and realize my would-be patriot, that personal defeat becomes bleak in front of the victory brought to humanity by you. Don't win as a person, do something to make humanity win. Take the steps beyond personal gain and personal pain, to bring victory upon humanity. Be the cause of humanity's joy – be the cause of humanity's cheer – be the cause of humanity's harmony – and above all be the cause of humanity's unification – even if it means walking on a road full of thorns every single day of your life.

Help humanity be human again – make humanity human again, because right now, it's anything but human. Today's humans are Christians, Jews, Muslims, Atheists, Liberals, Republicans and so many other things – they are everything but the one thing that matters more than anything else. In pursuit of sustaining the illusions of man-made identities, the humans have forgotten to be humans. Amidst this crisis and chaos of identities, those who can realize their biological identity of being human, have more practical metaphysics in them than all the mystics, preachers and philosophers in the world.

So, here the real question is not which identity is the greatest and highest among them all – to screw or not to screw this world, that's the question. Because, by taking labels of identity to be more significant than human life, we would only make a mess of this world, like we have done so far. So, now is the time, that we move away from that self-destructive path. Now is the time that we walk as humans and not as labels. Rise and walk, like did Rosa Parks, MLK, Madiba (Mandela), Honest Abe (Lincoln), Mevlana (Rumi) and many more. They did their part – I am doing mine – now it's your turn.

Article I
The Human Religion

Section 1. As the first step towards a dogma-less society, "human" will be added as a religious view on government records of citizens.

Section 2. Upon birth, a child's religion on paper would be that of the guardian, and once the child crosses the minor age barrier in the nation, he or she can change religion any time, simply by submitting an application at his or her local municipality, with a government issued proof of identity. Parental consent won't be necessary in the application process, as they themselves may feel hesitant to let their child change religion.

Section 3. A special "Religion Alteration Cell" will be erected in each state by the national government to carry out the religion alteration process without delay and, if requested by the applicant, to ensure that the applicant does not come to any harm throughout the process and until one year after the completion of the process.

The officials involved in the religion alteration of a citizen, should always refrain from using the terms "conversion" and "convert" on paper as well as in communication. Though humanity takes words for granted, every word induces certain sentimental significance in the human mind. The nature and intensity of that significance differ from word to word. "Conversion" and "convert" are among the words with intense negative sentimental significance. And the "fundamentalist" portion of the population will do everything in its power to use those words at their advantage to dishonor the "religion alteration process". Hence comes the next article of this constitution.

Article II
Science Awareness Program

Section 1. A Science Awareness Program will be made mandatory in all sectors of the society, including education, government and non-government sectors, with special attention to students.

Section 2. All schools will have the special science awareness program in all grades starting from fourth grade, where kids will be made aware of essential scientifically proven phenomena of the world along with the harms of quackery, superstitions, conspiracy theories and pseudoscience. For this purpose, at least once a month, the schools will invite a prominent scholar, local/non-local, to give a talk in the class.

Section 3. This will be a form of community service for the scholars, so no economic interest will be involved in the side of the school as well as the speaker.

Section 4. Religious stories that have not been academically proven to be historically accurate, can be taught in schools only as cultural myths, but not as historical facts.

Religion, Politics & Education – all three are exclusive feats of the human mind. Religion, when realized truly, can provide an extremely effective and evolving moral compass to the human conscience, while politics on the other hand, when utilized properly can ensure the wellbeing of the society. The real purpose of both is to serve humanity, yet we find ourselves in a situation, where both religious and political communities fight among each other in the pursuit of, not the service of the people, rather, the nourishment of the primordial element of personal superiority.

As a result, the primitive poison of authoritarianism from the fundamentalist part of both religion and politics has invaded all aspects of human life in the society, including the sacred domain of education. At a very early age, instead of nourishing the flourishing young minds of the kids, religious fundamentalism, assisted by political authoritarianism gloriously manages to compel the education system to teach the students Creationism.

The teachers of this system who are the second most important guides in the children's lives after their parents, either willingly or unwillingly teach a mythical story from the Book of Genesis of the Old Testament, as historical fact.

The most sensitive period of their developmental age, when the kids are supposed to be taught to question everything and nourish their reasoning skills, they are taught that God created the world in seven days – that the human race did not evolve from apes through millions of years, rather it came from the amorous congress between two God-made humans, named Adam and Eve. And if you ask why? The answers of the uneducated primordial teachers would be that the good book says so. And now if you ask, can't the scripture be wrong – do I have to take these stories literally? They would lash out with rage and shout at you – how dare you question the good book! Every single word in it is true. There is no greater truth than the truth of the good book.

In the hands of thinking humanity, religion can become one of the greatest tools to build a better world. But, until thinking humanity realizes the true meaning of religion in its heart, theoretical religion must be kept strictly outside the developmental years of the education system, especially till the finishing of the elementary school.

In the pursuit of excellence, religion can be a great aid to humanity. But the religion I am talking about here, is not the one with doctrines. Excellence doesn't come by obeying doctrines. Excellence comes through recognizing the flaws in the prevailing doctrines of the society and throwing them away if necessary, in the path of progress.

Science proceeds in exactly this manner, through constant questioning and analyzing the predominant scientific laws and modifying them if necessary. If science, as the most advanced tool in the hands of rational humanity can have the guts to change itself based on the needs of the time and society, why can't religion as the most influential tool in the hands of divine humanity, modify itself?

Science and Religion are two vividly different realms of the human mind. They work differently at the molecular level, but the purpose of both is alleviation of the Mind from the darkness of ignorance. Hence, only a fool would attempt to destroy one to ensure the triumph of the other. For a truly fascinating and healthy future of humanity to rise, these two distinct faculties of the human mind must assimilate the goodness of each other. One shall enrich the other, in the ultimate pursuit of the truth, progress and harmony.

Article III
Fundamentalism as Discrimination

Section 1. Religious fundamentalism is to be treated the same way, racism is treated. And this would be the first step towards eradicating terrorism, for fundamentalism is the main fuel for terrorism. And when the time is right, religious fundamentalism will be made a criminal offence.

However, at our current evolutionary stage, such an act would only appear as tyranny to many, so urgent steps will be taken by the government of each nation to raise awareness against religious fundamentalism, especially through humanitarian efforts, so that one day, all nations will come together to ban religious fundamentalism all together.

Section 2. A special task force will be created in each nation, comprising leading humanitarian thinkers of that nation, to raise awareness against fundamentalism, racism, bigotry and anti-intellectualism, through talks and humanitarian activities. Its purpose would be not to convert people's religious beliefs, but simply to make them see the harms of all sorts of segregation, discrimination and prejudices.

There is a basic terrorist germ in fundamentalism – a germ that is purely genocidal. This germ drives the psyche of mentally unstable individuals in the path of chaos, which is presented to them by the fundamentalists as the path of God. Without fundamentalism, terrorism won't exist in such an extreme form. All the violence in the name of God and religion shall stop festering, once the true essence of religion is realized in the heart of humans.

To the ill-minded representatives of theoretical religion, all other humans who do not follow their delusional ideology as the ultimate religion, are not just object of extreme detestation, they are, at the worst, lesser humans of false religions, who will be punished by God in hell after they die. And the only way to avoid being roasted in hell is to accept their God as the only true God. Therefore you see, talking reason with a fundamentalist is like talking balanced diet with a hungry tiger - you can't win.

This is not religion my friend. This is primitiveness at its worst. This is plain insanity. The more fundamentalist a person, the more immoral, inhuman and downright insane he or she becomes. Insanity is not healthy, especially when one insane idiot tries to impose his or her delusions on others. And the result is a species infested with baseless internal battles, many in the name of religion, yet, without actually having any true element of religion involved.

Here some might say, why not ban religion all together! Banning religion would mean taking away a part of people's identity - and regardless of what the atheist portion of the society "believes", taking away something so valuable from people is not a humane thing to do, for it is more important to be kind than right. People are more important than doctrines as well as truth - people can exist without truth, but truth can't exist without people.

So, let's have some humble patience for those who need their religion, as much as they need food, water and air, until we actually succeed in building a global community, where people can rely on people and do not need the organized walls of religion to take shelter in, in times of distress.

Section 3. And at the same time, we must make efforts to diminish the authoritarian power of religious institutions over the society. So, as the first measure, religious institutions will not be tax exempt.

Article IV
Quackery, Pseudoscience and Healthcare

Section 1. Practice of quackery in any form, that does direct harm to human health such as exorcism, will be punishable by the Court System of a nation.

Section 2. If any of the alternative treatments/medicines is found to have direct harmful impact on human health, necessary actions will be taken immediately to ban such practice in the nation where it is found to be harmful, upon proper investigation carried out by a team of medical doctors. All investigations on this matter will be monitored by the national wing of WHO. And the national government will take immediate actions on the conclusions of WHO.

Section 3. Also, all faith-healing communions will be monitored by a MD appointed by the national WHO.

Section 4. FDA will have the right to ban the manufacturing, distribution and selling of any pseudo-scientific or quackery product in any country, if they see it to be a direct threat to human health.

Article V
Firearms Control

Section 1. Civilians will not be permitted to possess firearms of any kind, except with proper license, which can only be received by providing evidence of possible threat to their safety.

Section 2. If the evidence checks out, the applicant must go through extensive firearms training before having the license for firearm.

Here possessing firearms is not the issue, rather the issue is the sense of responsibility, without which, possessing a firearm doesn't make a positive difference whatsoever, but only harms serenity in a community. The masses with firearms are like newborns with knives. Such power in the hands of the common people doesn't ensure security in any manner, rather it only jeopardizes security of the self as well as others.

Firearms can't ensure safety in the society, only open arms can. So, open your arms to the helpless, and be the real guardian angel to those in need, because if you don't stand up for humanity, no other supernatural force is going to come and save humanity. All the help that humanity needs is vested in you by Mother Nature.

You are the heirs of infinite love and light. Come out my friend. Come out from the narrow lanes of darkness. Come out into the vivacious light of the day where all the glory resides. Come out, O my lion-heart sibling, and shake off the ancient mysticism and prejudices. You are the most fascinating expression of Mother Nature. Your soul is the expression of the whole Universe. All the power in the universe is born with you in your biology. Recognize them, realize them and ultimately utilize them in the pursuit of spreading love, harmony and peace, instead of spreading fear and violence in the name of self-defense. Keep in mind my friend, it's better to die in the hands of your own kind than from some ruthless disease. Give up your fear of death and no power will have authority over your life.

Article VI
Freedom of Press

Section 1. Traditional publishing houses and broadcasting studios will be exempt from content moderation, as long as they maintain their journalistic integrity by doing the necessary fact check for their stories.

Section 2. Journalism will have zero tolerance policy for fake content, quackery and pseudo-science, and broadcasting or publishing of such material, for example, astrology, psychics and others, in any manner, will be a punishable offence.

In practice, nothing changes for the traditional news media sector, except for the increased responsibility that they have to bear in order to deliver genuine evidence-based content to the audience. Journalism will only gain more importance over time, than it ever had in the past, because never in history, the society was so much saturated with false news. Now more than ever, journalists have a crucial role to perform in the society.

You may say, haven't they been playing that role from the very beginning! Yes, they have been doing it for a long time, since the birth of printing press, but never in history, could their failure mean devastation in their community caused by their false and illegitimate counterparts.

Before the printing press was invented, word of mouth was the primary source of news. Returning merchants, sailors and travelers brought news back to the mainland, and this was then picked up by peddlers and small time travelers and spread from town to town. But this form of news transmission was highly unreliable, for there was no way to distinguish rumor or half-truth from the truth. That came to a temporary halt with the invention of printing press.

Newspapers (and to a lesser extent magazines) have always been the primary medium of journalism since the 18th century, radio and television in the 20th century, and the Internet in the 21st century. However, more and more people are consuming news and other content from the internet than any other medium. And that's where the problem begins. The production and circulation of physical newspaper is highly expensive and so is maintaining a tv channel or a radio station, hence, transmission of news through these platforms are accessible mostly to traditional news media sources, and the public only acts as the consumer. But the same is not true when it comes to the transmission of news or any other content via the Internet. Anybody can transmit a news via the internet quite instantly as well as consume it. And since there is no active fact-checking algorithm involved in this transmission, there is no way of telling whether the news you are receiving is real or fake, if you are not receiving it from a trusted traditional source.

However, since most of the traditional news publishing industry is hugely dependent on corporate sponsorship (except for a few publishers funded by people), even their news can be manipulated for the benefit of the sponsors or political lobbies. So, in the end, it all comes down to journalistic integrity - it comes down to the ethical grounds of the real conscientious journalists.

Therefore, it again comes down to the matter of social trust upon the individual journalist, whose life purpose is to provide as much uninfluenced and unbiased information to the society as possible. The whole civilized world runs on trust - people trust journalists to provide accurate information, doctors to provide accurate treatment, scientists to provide accurate answers and solutions to unanswered questions and unsolved problems, pilots to provide safe and fast air transportation, and so on.

So, the integrity of the civilized world is predicated on the integrity of the individual in their chosen field of work. Upon their sense of responsibility depends the healthy functioning of an entire species. So, my brave and bold journalists, rise and work with integrity, for now more than ever, the world faces an imminent information-catastrophe, and you are our first line of defense. So, be the shield against disinformation and go down to the deepest and darkest pit to rescue the human society, from the strangling tendrils of mal-content. There is a lot to be done my friend, so don't be silent - make journalism the vanguard of information. Declare a peaceful intolerance of disinformation, quackery, conspiracy theories and pseudo-science.

Article VII
Content Moderation

Section 1. No content can bring such devastation in a person's life, as much as porn can, so to bring down the damage of porn done to the society by ruining lives, all pornsites will be legally required to make sure that no explicit material will be made live, without confirming the consent accompanied by identity proof, from the person/persons visible in the material, and failure to comply to this verification requirement would mean permanent shut down of the site.

Section 2. A special "Porn Control Wing" will be created in the Cybercrime department of a national government, to watch over the activity of pornsites.

Explicit material has been a key source of pleasure for the human civilization from the very beginning. But the time has come that we make sure, this specific form of entertainment doesn't ruin any life in the process, for any content, once made online, leaves an immortal footprint, which can rarely be erased completely. So, it must be made certain that the parties involved in the explicit content have all willingly consented to the publication of that content.

Section 3. All censorship on entertainment content should be accomplished by trained Neuroscientists/Psychologists/Psychiatrists only. The purpose of this is not to hamper free speech, but to ensure that the content does not have a negative impact on the society.

Before the invention of printing press, the problem was, lack of information, and now due to the rise of social media, it is too much information - the former leads to mental starvation and the latter to mental obesity. Both are lethal, so it becomes the responsibility of the creator of the medium to ensure that their creation does not lead humanity down the road of insanity.

Unfortunately, destination insanity is no longer an imminent possibility, rather we have already entered its territory. We have begun to live in a world, where we eat content, drink content and breathe content, without giving a single thought to its composition and what kind of impact it has upon our lives. Unmoderated content consumption is as dangerous as the consumption of sewage water.

To speak psycho-physiologically in this context, consumption of sewage water first ruins your physiological health, which may lead to psychological troubles, whereas consumption of unmoderated content, first quite radically ruins your psychological health, and in fact, your entire psychological existence, which is basically what you are, and then it eventually leads to a total catastrophe of your psycho-physiological existence.

However, we no longer have the luxury to simply wait till the major social media platforms come up with an actual content-moderation algorithm, for in the meantime, things would get worse. Hence, rises the necessity of the next section.

Section 4. Without actual content moderation, no social media platform will be legally permitted to present advertisements to users.

This is the most effective way to make the social media platforms take the issue of fake-content seriously. Social media giants have made billions in revenue from advertisements, by exploiting people's content addiction, and now is the time to put an end to this exploitation.

The focus of social media's business model must shift from content engagement to content quality. And the only way to measure quality of content is through an active content-moderation algorithm. The parameters of this content-moderation process should be devised, guided by a team of Neuroscientists/ Psychologists/ Psychiatrists.

It is practically impossible to moderate the gigantean amount of content uploaded on social media every minute, if it is to be done by humans. So, with the guidance of Neuroscientists/ Psychologists/ Psychiatrists, each social medial platform must at once, take the initiative to develop a functional algorithm to do the moderation effectively.

Freedom of expression on social media will be maintained for any user as long as their original posts do not contain misinformation, racism, xenophobia, fundamentalism, bigotry or any other form of primitive advocacy. Remember, facebook without content moderation is a gun without gun control. Here facebook or any other social platform, is the gun and information is the bullet - without proper, responsible usage, it will do more harm to the society than it'll do good. This is the sector where Artificial Intelligence should be brought to practice first, instead of childishly running after pompous ideas of singularity and sentient machines.

The problem with most smart people is that they are too dumb to distinguish necessity from luxury, that's why despite having the resources to deal with real problems that cause misery to humanity, they keep wasting those resources on pompous dreams. And you can have first-hand experience with such stupidity if you visit any CES event. Whether it is smart toilet or smart underwear, there is no end to intellectual, wealthy and pompous stupidity. Silicon Valley is no longer the valley of innovators who solve problems, it has turned into the valley of resourceful stupidity. They are a bunch of people wasting resources on creating products that do nothing more than fuel the predominant neurosis of consumerism. If an innovation doesn't solve a problem, it's an innovation that you can live without.

Now we must ask the question, what is a problem? For example, darkness is a problem, so when Edison supposedly invented the first light bulb, it allowed humanity to cross a great hurdle in the path of progress. But then arose the problem of delivering power to all the light bulbs in a country across great distance, for which Edison had to develop many power stations nation-wide, because his Direct Current was not able to travel long distance without loss of power. This specific problem was then solved by Nikola Tesla, through his idea of Alternating Current, which till this day, powers the entire world.

Then there was another problem - the problem of conveying message from one place to another swiftly - this problem was somewhat solved by the use of messenger pigeon. But they were still not fast enough. And this grand problem of long-distance communication was again solved by Tesla, as he invented the first wireless communication between devices. Two of humanity's greatest technological achievements were made by Tesla, yet he remains hugely unrecognized outside the scientific and geek circle. So, I hereby propose (to the United

Nations) that 10th of July, the birthday of Nikola Tesla be recognized as International Invention Day.

Now to get back to the matter in hand, Artificial Intelligence can provide peer-less assistance to human progress, but only as artificial intelligence, not as artificial sentience. Here what you must understand is that, intelligence is not equivalent to sentience. For example, imagine that you enter a competition of chess. Now imagine what happens if you emerge as the winner - imagine the happiness in the heart of your friends and family - imagine all the glory that your winning would bring both in your own mind as well as in your community - and the same can happen with a sad tone if you lose the game. Now imagine what happens if an AI program wins the game over you. You as well as your friends and family would be sad because you lost, but the winner, i.e. the AI itself will not even be aware of the fact that it has won - rather, winning would only be a matter of historical record in its data storage without any emotional significance whatsoever.

And such AI already exists, developed to play board games. For example, Alpha-Go is an AI program developed by Google Deepmind, to play the board game Go. Alpha-Go has already defeated the Korean grandmaster Lee Sedol, becoming the first machine to beat a professional player and it went on to win against the world number one, Ke Jie, in China.

The point is, for the humans winning or losing accompanies a cascade of emotional reactions, whereas, for a machine, winning or losing means nothing except for pieces of factual data. This is exactly where lies the distinction between weak AI and strong AI. To explain it simply, a sentient AI is called strong AI, and a non-sentient AI, is referred to as weak AI. All we have till this day in the form of AI is weak AI.

No matter how intelligent a machine is made, it will always be a weak AI. However, if artificial intelligence does develop some kind of sentience or self-awareness at some point in the distant future, it will happen quite suddenly, without any prior warning, and quite instantly, humans will no longer be the masters of this planet.

Being sentient, such a machine could step beyond the limitations of the algorithms programmed in it by its creator, and therefore it will no longer need an inferior species called the humans. Hence humans will become, to such a sentient computer, what an ant is today to us. We don't necessarily hate an ant, but if it's in our way, squashing it is not a big deal. Similar will be the future of humanity in a world of sentient machines. They will not necessarily hate us, but they will not love us either, to hail human life of more importance than their own needs.

Let me elaborate a bit further - killing a living creature for its meat is surely a morally degrading act, yet we don't mind eating meat, despite the fact that we don't hate the creature whose meat we are eating. Likewise, a sentient machine won't exactly hate us, but they won't love us either, any more than we love fish or chicken. However, artificial intelligence is nowhere near attaining that kind of actual sentience or awareness. And without awareness it's simply a mechanical device, which may pretend to show emotions and sentience, if it is programmed to do so, and thus it may be able to fool the humans as being alive, but in its own internal circuitry, it'd simply be following its preprogrammed tasks through the flowchart of an algorithm.

At the current stage of our technological development, we can indeed create an artificial intelligence that can almost succeed in fooling the majority of the humans with its pre-programmed pretenses that it is sentient, but pretending to have sentience is not the same as showing signs of sentience. For example, Alexa or Siri may sound quite alive to many, but it's simply following instructions on some algorithm, and is not even aware of its own actions.

Human mind on the other hand, is not a complex mechanical device, yet most humans act exactly like one – following a certain set of conformities – some of those conformities get programmed in the human brain by the society, in the form of acceptable norms, and others are instinctual in nature, such as racial attitude, which is born from either conscious or subconscious loyalty to one's own group. Such group loyalty helped our primal ancestors in the jungle to stay strong together in a tribe, which increased their chances of survival against threats from predators or other tribes.

All these psychological traits are programmed by Mother Nature in all of us, and they can easily kick in, if the necessity arises. Now the reason that some humans don't act racists, is because they have succeeded in taking the step beyond their innate programming with the use of their higher mental functioning. Computers are programmed, so are the humans, but the computers can't act outside their programming, whereas the humans can. That's where the vivid distinction between a sentient human and a non-sentient computer lies. And that is why, Artificial Intelligence can be a supplement to human insight, not substitute - it can be an aid to human existence, but not a replacement.

Article VIII
Animal Welfare

Our theoretical and practical parameters of morality are hugely based on our needs. Having said that, let's now place our focus on the issue of animal welfare and rights, since we made a little mention about meat eating in the last article. To put it simply, is it right to eat meat or not, that's the question. The question here may sound easy, but the answer is not so simple. Of course, it's not right to eat meat, since we are killing those creatures for their flesh, but things are more complicated than that.

If we take into account the actual health aspect of not eating meat in the human society then, what I must point out is that, vegan diet is not necessarily healthy, but it does have the moral high ground. However, at the very least, the humans must attempt to not aid in the extinction of any species, hence rises the first section of this article.

Section 1. Consumption of meat from endangered species in a country will be banned by the national government in that country.

Some scientists are already working to fix the moral dilemma that comes along with eating meat, by developing artificial meat. Research into developing artificial meat or to be more accurate, "cultured meat" or "in vitro meat" is advancing greatly. And here you must remember that, though it is often called artificial meat, it is not fully artificial, by its origin.

Cultured meat is developed from stem cells that are extracted from healthy animal sources. The process by which cultured meat is created is called tissue engineering and it originated in the field of regenerative medicine. For the process of producing cultured meat, muscle stem cells are taken from a donor organism in a muscle biopsy, and are then proliferated in-vitro at the laboratory. The cells are cultivated in growth media using matrices, where they multiply (proliferation). Finally, the stem cells grow into muscle cells (differentiation), which then turn into muscle fibers.

Meat is a mixture of skeletal muscle, fat tissue and supportive tissues such as connective tissue. Stem cells of each of these tissues can be harvested from animals and multiplied to such an extent that a small sample can be multiplied into industrial quantities of meat, thus vastly reducing the number of animals that need to be raised, fed and slaughtered to satisfy consumer demand.

Now the point is, cultured meat has already been successfully developed in the lab, but large-scale production will take at least a few decades. This is owed largely to the fact that the basic components of a cultured meat process need to be researched in more depth. Among other issues, the production of cultured meat requires suitable cells, an appropriate growth medium (ideally non-animal in origin, because animal components can contain communicable diseases), suitable (edible) materials for the matrices (e.g. fibrin-hydrogen gel), along which the cells can grow to produce thicker pieces of meat.

In short, cultured meat holds a sustainable, healthier and a bit more moral future for humanity. Two of the greatest blessings of cultured meat are animal welfare and human health. The literature on the subject indicates the vision that a single animal might be enough to satisfy the worldwide need for meat. Even if such an idea is an exaggeration, it is still conceivable that the reduced number of animals could make factory farming obsolete, resulting in better living conditions for the few animals still needed. Also, the most important factor here is that, as the process attains perfection, no animal would actually have to be killed to obtain stem cells. Cultured meat is also healthier, because it is produced in the laboratory under controlled conditions.

Basically, a beautiful, organic future is on the cards for humanity, as far as food consumption is concerned. However, you must also remember that, we will still require animals for trials of drugs. And definitely this also counts as animal cruelty, but we don't live in a world of perfect non-violent beauty. If we don't do the trials on animal specimens first, would you rather give yourself or a relative of yours up for experimentation!

Some may say, why don't we avoid experimentation on live specimens all together - to them I say, modern medicine is not magic to work without errors - and hard and cruel as it may sound, a live animal specimen is expendable, but not a live human being. You may say, that's not fair - and indeed, it is in no way fair, but that's the reality. The only fairer alternative is to let humans suffer and die from diseases, like they used to, until about a few centuries ago.

In short, there is no right choice here, but only a less cruel choice, where, though we take human rights to be of utmost importance, we also take animal welfare into consideration. At our current stage of scientific development in various fields, human rights and animal rights cannot go hand in hand, we must compromise one to benefit the other. From a conscientious standpoint, use of animals is morally wrong, but we can't avoid it if we are to ensure human wellbeing, at least not yet. We don't yet have the moral luxury to give importance to animal rights over human rights - it's no doubt a great idea, but not practical, not just yet.

However, what we can do is, eliminate unnecessary animal cruelty, which is the very purpose of animal welfare initiatives. For example, a recent documentary entitled "Love and Bananas", directed and produced by my inspired friend Ashley Michael Bell, captures such an animal welfare initiative in Thailand, in a bold, beautiful and awe-inspiring fashion, where she helps rescue a 70 years old captive elephant. Such magnificent animal welfare initiatives are taking place all over the world.

However, I must also mention that many of the activists go so far in the path of animal welfare, that they enter the domain of animal rights activism, where they resort to all sorts of anti-humanitarian atrocities to protect animal rights over human rights. The existential fact is, we do need to use animals compromising their right to live, if we are to sustain health and welfare in human life, but we can reduce that consumption to a great extent. For example, you can avoid clothing that are made by slaughtering animals. We need animals for food, because vegan diet is not necessarily healthy, as I said earlier, but the same is not true for clothing. We do use animals for clothing, but we don't need to. We could do just fine with non-animal and non-cruel clothing and other apparels.

Article IX
Electoral Entrance Examination

Section 1. Electoral candidate submissions will be accepted only after the candidates pass the "Electoral Entrance Examination" or EEE. EEE will be an extensive nation-wide Psych-Eval Test concocted by a team of Psychologists/ Psychiatrists, with the purpose of evaluating the candidate's reasoning skills, biases, views on inclusion and diversity, and decision-making skills. Upon passing the EEE, the candidates will be given "License for Political Practice".

EEE test will be devised in a way that it evaluates the candidate's genuine views and skills, without the candidate being aware, which question evaluates what kind of view - and the purpose of EEE is not to evaluate whether a candidate is intelligent, rather it is to evaluate whether he or she possesses any overwhelming and harmful cognitive deficit such as bigotry, misogyny and fundamentalism.

Section 2. Candidates who fail to pass the EEE, may again take the exam after five years.

Section 3. If a celebrity from the entertainment industry chooses to sit for EEE, and thereafter wins the election, he or she would no longer engage in content creation activity of the entertainment industry, except for in special initiatives to raise public awareness on social issues, all profits from which, if any, would be utilized for the people of the territory in which the representative is active.

Now, we must investigate in brief, the necessity of Electoral Entrance Examination. Let's begin with a question. If your spouse gets sick, who would you visit - your non-doctor neighbor or an actual doctor! Any sane person would visit a doctor over a non-doctor neighbor, even if that neighbor happens to be a celebrity, because it is common knowledge that fame or charisma is not equivalent to medical expertise, yet when it comes to choosing a doctor to treat the sickness of a nation, the masses most proudly elect any charismatic chimpanzee over a humble, wise and conscientious leader.

If this is democracy then the first responsibility of a government is to make immediate amendments to that democracy. And the most effective way to do that is to take political leadership seriously, just like any other technical profession, such as medical practice, scientific research or pilot-hood. And in order to do this efficiently, a nation must get its candidates evaluated through EEE, before they go out in the world to become would-be leaders of a people.

This is the only way to make sure that no matter how bad the choice of the majority is, they don't at the very least choose a leader who could essentially impede progress, harmony and assimilation in the human society. This is the only way we could make sure that the candidates the people choose from, have been properly tested by professionals, just like a doctor gets properly evaluated before having their license to practice medicine. If a nation gets sick, the citizens must be able to make their choice of leader among candidates who possess a functional conscientious mind to determine the fate of an entire people, or else, the world will end up with more walls and prisons than bridges.

Section 4. And last but not the least, in order to ensure proper progressive, non-prejudicial and non-barbarian functioning of a government, on top of the government hierarchy, in each nation, all political activities will be monitored and guided by a group of scholars, comprising scientists and philosophers.

Article X
Evidence-based Lawmaking

Section 1. All proposed laws and bills must pass the evaluation by a team of scientists and philosophers.

Science and Philosophy should be the collective foundation of lawmaking. Here the science part is easy - it simply means taking the conviction of the majority of scientists as gospel. But when it comes to philosophy, things get a bit complicated, because people often take any famous actor or artist as a philosopher.

All opinions are not equal, as far as running a people is concerned. If the plumbing of my house isn't working, then I'd call a plumber, not a doctor or a physicist. If I have a question about the universe, I would ask a physicist and not a plumber or a doctor, and if I have an ailment, I'd seek treatment from a doctor, not a physicist or a plumber. It makes people feel good to say that all opinions are equal, because somehow, they correlate equality of opinions with equality of human dignity. And that's exactly where lies one of the most disgraceful and harmful perceptual errors of the society, that leads to an unfit government.

A plumber's opinion about the universe is way inferior than that of a physicist, but that doesn't make the plumber inferior to a physicist. Likewise, a physicist's opinion about plumbing is way inferior to that of a plumber, but that doesn't make the physicist an inferior being. The problem is, the society uses profession as the measure of the person, while in reality, the only way to measure a person is through his or her behavior with other people. No one is inferior to no one.

All humans are equal, but not everyone has the mental capacity to decide what's best for harmony and progress of a people. Exactly for this reason, all laws and bills that would essentially determine the fate of a people, must pass the scrutiny of a bunch of scientists and actual scholarly philosophers first. The best option would be if scientists and philosophers forged the laws and bills with their own hands themselves, but that would mean engaging full time in the making of laws and bills, while monitoring their actualization in the field, which would cut them off from their actual field of work.

Section 2. Scientists and philosophers must be able to scrutinize the laws and bills without any conflict of interest and without losing touch with their actual field of work.

What you call law is essentially the need of an uncivilized and unfree society. A truly civilized and free society needs no law. The presence of law is not the sign of order, but it is the sign of disorder. Hence, the true purpose of law should not be to maintain order, rather it should be to create a truly lawless society. Order lies in lawlessness, whereas in law lies disorder.

So, does this mean, we should get rid of law all together! Before we attempt to investigate the answer to this question, we must first understand what law really is and what kind of impact it has upon the internal realm of the human society. Law is an illusory perceptual structure - a pattern, built by humans to depict the acceptable and non-acceptable behavior of humans in a certain society. This structure defines for all humans in a specific society, what is right and what is wrong.

Now the question is, on what grounds does law define the righteousness of its own depictions! Lawmakers, who rarely have an insight of a truly progressive and civilized society, decide on the perimeters of law based on their biases and knacks, and rarely on actual scientific evidence. It's like asking the blind to show the path. So, for law to be of actual use in the society at our current evolutionary stage, it must be cooked in the vessel of scientific findings with the fire of reasoning and compassion. And once they are cooked, they will be presented to the master chef of progress, i.e. a team of scientists and philosophers for the final judgement on whether or not they will be delivered to the people.

Article XI
Gender Equality Everywhere

Section 1. A cabinet of ministers will have equal numbers of male and female members.

Men have been running the world from the very beginning, and hard as it may sound, they haven't exactly done it well, that's because one of the archetypal traits of male character is aggression, which enabled our primitive grandfathers acquire food and protect their mates and offspring. The female psychology however is a bit different. Harmony runs through their nerves, except for a few monthly hiccups that most women learn to have a handle on quite efficiently.

All the bloodsheds in human history have been caused by men, not women. And there is a biological reason for this. As boys grow up to become men, testosterone becomes a major driving force behind their innate urge to have authority over their environment. Aggression and rage both serve as crucial emotional and behavioral expressions to satisfy that need for authority.

The female brain is engineered by Mother Nature to avoid conflicts at all cost, whereas the male brain pleasures conflicts in the purpose of having authority. Women are motivated on a molecular level to ease and even prevent social conflicts. Maintaining a smooth inter-personal relationship at all costs is the female brain's primary goal.

The female brain has a far more negative alert reaction to relationship conflict and rejection than does the male brain. Men often relish interpersonal conflict and competition. They even get a positive psychological boost from it. In women, conflict is more likely to set in motion a cascade of negative neurochemical reactions, creating feelings of stress and fear. Just the thought of a possible imminent conflict can be read by the female brain as a threat to the relationship and hence can give rise to serious concerns. That's why women are neurologically more capable of keeping their rage in control than men, so that it doesn't hamper any of their interpersonal relationships in the society.

Studies have shown that though men and women say that they feel anger for an equal number of minutes per day, men get physically aggressive twenty times more often than women. Due to the abundance of testosterone receptors in the amygdala, high testosterone level makes it even more difficult for a man to tame his rage and aggression, than a woman. Other than testosterone, a man's brain circuit for aggression is highly influenced by vasopressin, cortisol and adrenalin. And in most cases when a man's anger reaches the boiling point, it gives him an utter sensation of pleasure. The pleasure of utter aggression further motivates a man to win the fight.

All these are evolutionarily encoded inside the male brain to ensure the survival of the progeny and the mate at all cost. But in today's world, this male trait ends up doing more harm than good. The neurologically encoded primitive instinct of aggression, rising from the amygdala, often finds its way out in modern situations and quite subconsciously compels the men to act as if they are in the environment of the wild.

In an adult human brain, the male amygdala is significantly larger than the female amygdala, even when total brain size is taken into consideration. While on the contrary women have slightly larger prefrontal cortex and anterior cingulate cortex that are involved in controlling the rage and avoiding any kind of conflict. As a result, women in general have better hold of their anger response than men. All men either consciously or subconsciously crave for authority over their environment, especially over their peers in the society, male and female alike. Women on the other hand, crave for intimacy especially from their female peers in the society. Colloquially this is what you call "gossiping".

Now one might wonder, why do women spend so much time in talking to their female peers? The answer can again be found in the process of biological evolution of the human mind. Just like the evolutionary expression of aggression in men, gossiping is an evolutionary feature of the female psychology. Women trade various secrets from their personal experiences through gossiping in order to create connection and intimacy with their female peers. By doing this, what they are accomplishing is the development of close-knit cliques with secret rules. In these new groups, talking, telling secrets, and gossiping, in fact, often become women's favorite activities - their tools to navigate and ease the ups and downs and stresses of life.

Connecting through talking activates the pleasure centers in a woman's brain. Here I'm not talking about a small amount of pleasure. This is huge. It's a major dopamine and oxytocin rush, which is the biggest, fattest and extremely substantial neurological reward you can get outside of an orgasm. Dopamine stimulates the motivation and pleasure circuits in the brain, while Oxytocin triggers a sense of intimacy. The combination of dopamine and oxytocin forms the biological basis of the female drive for intimacy with its stress-reducing effect.

Thus, women are driven by a desire for connection with their peers in the society. Their dopamine and oxytocin rush from talking and connecting keeps them motivated to seek out these intimate connections. But this is typically a girl thing – an exclusive reality of the female mental universe. Now imagine, what happens when you put such a fantastic trait into practice in the pursuit of resolving the giant conflicts of the society. That's the best thing that can ever happen to this world.

Evolutionarily speaking, conflict-resolution is a fundamental mental faculty of women, way beyond the wildest imaginations of any man. So, it is high time that gender equality is made a legal requirement of the cabinet that runs a nation. For a society to truly progress, we don't need woman or man, we need a fully-fledged human - nothing short of that would do.

In the progressive society of thinking humanity, gender equality is not something you believe in, it is a quintessential part of human existence. Do not forget my friend, the future of human civilization is predicated on the quality of human existence, not just the quality of male existence. I am saying again, gender equality is not a belief, it is not an idea - it is a key element of the society that will define whether we the humans shall march ahead towards glory and advancement, or sink into the abyss of an existential doom.

Hence, the first step, we must take is, sever the obvious association between femininity and sexuality in the psyche of the society. How dare the society calls itself civilized, while hailing women first as sexual objects, then as everything else! How dare a man foster the primitive courage to hit on every woman he encounters, as if she has been waiting her whole life to be hit on – as if to be hit on, is the purpose of her existence! Rise, my brothers, and see women as persons, and not as objects of sexual gratification. And if you are single, and truly would like to be with a woman you like, then be a gentleman and ask her out with respect, instead of treating her as an object to possess.

In a world where female existence is confused with sexual gratification, even the maternal gesture of breastfeeding appears to be an act of sexually predatory behavior to the ill-minded. Remember, where women are respected, there flourishes civilization.

The whole human world is born from the womb of mothers, and if we can't make the motherly act of breast-feeding free from stigma in such a world, then it's an insult to our very existence as a species. Remember, being able to breastfeed at any place in the society, is not a privilege of the women, rather it's a privilege of civilized humanity.

It is true that breasts can induce sexual tension in men, but truer than that is the fact, that breasts are the primary and healthiest source of nutrition for the infant, so, if men can't use their higher mental faculty of self-restraint at the sight of breastfeeding at public places, then it's not the women who need to change their breastfeeding place, it's the men who need to work on their character. An animal without character is merely animal, but a human without character is worse than animal, because the animals don't have the brain capacity to foster a sense of character, whereas the humans do.

Character is what distinguishes us from the animals - it makes us human in the functional sense of the term, not just in the theoretical sense. Theory and functionality are two completely different things. For example, in theory, feminism means advocacy of women's rights in a world that still hugely runs by the force of patriarchy, but when we actually begin to investigate the actual functional reality of this concept of feminism, we find something rather ugly, that's far from the humane advocacy of women's rights - we find that in the name of feminism, the so-called advocates of women's rights, especially the famous ones, confuse public eroticism to be the expression of female empowerment. Feminism means standing up for women's rights, not reinforcing the society's perception of women as objects for sexual gratification, by advocating for public eroticism.

Likewise, in theory, humanism means to advocate for human rights, above and beyond all labels of religion and race, but in practice, many of the so-called humanists take anti-religiousness to be the same as advocacy of humanism. A huge portion of the human population needs religion as much as they need food and water. And anyone who doesn't recognize this simple reality of human frailty, is neither a humanist, nor a being of conscience.

So, you see, all the glorious ideas of the civilized human society have two sides, one is the theoretical or conceptual side and the other is the functional or practical side. Many of the problems of this world are caused by our instinctive urge to focus all our attention on the theoretical side without actually giving any attention on its practical implications. The point is, when you start acting as a real, conscientious and liberated human, then and then only can you see both the healthy and harmful sides of all the ideas in the world.

Article XII
Land Dispute between Nations

Section 1. In case of land dispute between two nations, proper investigation is to be made by United Nations, in the hands of social scientists, not from those two countries, upon the actual living conditions of the citizens of that specific land, and based on the investigation, all efforts will be made to improve the living conditions of the citizens without separating the land from its current country.

Section 2. In extreme circumstances, an experiment will be done on the land, by announcing the joint ownership of the land by two of those countries and all efforts will be made to ensure peace and harmony in that region for five years.

Section 3. If the experiment fails to ensure peace and harmony in that five years duration, that land will be officially made a part of the country where the citizens of that land would feel safest.

Article XIII
Global Ownership of Nuclear Weapons

Section 1. All the countries of Planet Earth will have collective ownership of any nuclear weapon developed by any country.

Section 2. And the use of the nuclear weapon, when the need arises, will require majority consent from scientists representing their countries.

On a cursory view, it may appear to many that banning of nuclear weapons would be best for our planet, but that is not exactly true. Nuclear weapons are not exactly the problem here, the real problem is humanity's incapability to use it for the good of entire humanity. Nukes are no more cause for concern than knives and hammers are - it is our awareness of their right use that determines whether they would bring destruction upon the world or become the last line of defense for the human species, if and when the need arises.

The mother can use a knife in the kitchen to chop vegetables and make a healthy meal, but if you give a knife to a child and the child accidentally injures himself, is it the fault of the knife! The same is with us humans and our nukes. However, we can't also deny the fact that nuclear weapons have the highest potential to destroy a great number of people, and that is why, no one nation would hold the exclusive ownership of such great power. No matter which country develops it, nuclear weapon developed in any corner of the world would be the collective possession of all countries.

Article XIV
Climate Change as Human Rights Issue

Climate change is a human rights infringement - also it is a criminal offence, because by not taking action to fix it, a citizen would be essentially committing homicide of countless citizens of the future.

Section 1. Therefore, climate change will be dealt with as a human rights issue.

I am pain-stricken to say, the human society has been obsessed with entertainment for so long, that they have almost gone blind to the obvious signs of distress that Mother Earth has been sending for decades. And the signs have become more and more intense and agonizing these recent few decades. Still, you do not see it, or even if you do, you just wash it off your head as just another freak weather scenario.

But, let me tell you – extreme weather events have started to take place throughout the world – rainfall is getting heavier and lasting longer. Hurricanes and Typhoons are becoming more intense and destructive with stronger winds, as the planet, especially our oceans, continues to get warmer.

Average global sea surface temperatures are rising, and as sea surface temperatures become warmer, hurricanes become more powerful. Warmer oceans, and especially increased deep ocean warmth, also fuel rapid intensification of storms, so a once-relatively weak storm can cross the right stretch of water and become major in a matter of hours. This can lead to citizens being under-prepared for the intensity of the actual hurricane that makes landfall, resulting in greater damage and even loss of life. As the world becomes warmer, more water evaporates from the surface of our oceans. Hurricanes suck up this water vapor as they travel over the sea surface, and when they make landfall, the same water vapor returns to the earth's surface as heavy precipitation.

When water evaporates from the land and sea, it eventually returns to Earth as rain and snow. Climate change intensifies this cycle because as air temperatures increase, more water evaporates into the air.

Because warmer air holds more water vapor, this is contributing to an increase in the average annual amount of rain and snow in some places and creating more intense rainstorms in others. The result is a whole lot of major problems, like extreme storm and flooding in communities around the world. The most recent horrible example that comes to my mind is Hurricane Florence.

Additionally, at the same time, sea levels are rising faster than at any time in almost 3,000 years, and it's worsening coastal flooding globally. The United Nations Environmental Programme estimates that half of the world's population lives within 60 kilometers of a coast – and three-quarters of all major cities are on a shoreline. Now here is the irony of the issue – we scientists predicted all this long ago, and now we are seeing it play out in front of our eyes, because our previous generations were too idiot to recognize the signs of Nature as well as the warnings of scientists. Now my question to you is, are you as idiot and as irresponsible as our ancestors? Don't you have any responsibility towards your children and their children?

Providing food, shelter, clothing and education is not enough any more, because all of this would have no meaning in the end, if your children do not have a planet to live on with health and prosperity.

17 of the 18 hottest years on record have occurred this century. As the planet gets warmer, we are going to have more intense and frequent heat waves, which would in turn increase the rate of death from illnesses as well, like heart attack, heat stroke, organ failure, and others. So, the point is, disasters are going to get more and more frequent on this planet – this is a fact – a fact as clear and radiant as the sun in the sky. And all of it is happening because the planet is getting warmer, basically due to the childish and sometimes uncivilized actions of the humans. The green-house gas emission caused by us is the main ingredient in the poisonous cocktail of global warming which will eventually destroy your children.

Now Let me give you an example. Imagine there is a bottle of poison on the desk. What do you think will happen, if you bring the bottle down and drink the poison! You know the answer right! You see it as a fact, that if you drink it, you surely will bid goodbye to life. Similar is the matter of global warming. If you stay indifferent and don't act to treat it, then it's your descendants who shall have to bid goodbye to their life.

Global warming is happening right at this very moment, as you are reading this constitution – deal with it. It's not a prediction or a matter of the future any more. And some of you may think that, there's nothing to worry, for all humans will eventually move to MARS. Well, here is the news for you. Science does not yet have the means to colonize an entire planet and make it suitable for human living, no matter how much some privately owned space agencies boast about it. Also, when we actually develop the technology to visit MARS, may be in a century or perhaps more, the trip is not going to be available to everyone. Only the richest will get a chance, to simply visit MARS, and not to live there. To actually live on MARS, it'll take many millennia. So, for the countless millennia to come, Mother Earth is going to be our only place to live – the place called home.

Now here is a shocking fact, since Earth is our only home, which is actually currently in danger, in the coming centuries, this only home is going to become less and less suitable for living. Hence, your children and their children will have nowhere to go. The only factual future that awaits your progeny, is a horrible death. All because you do not feel responsible enough to take actions to treat the damaged home you live in. You will die after living a comfortable life, but the life of your kids and grandkids will be full of misery, because, you think, global warming is not an urgent enough issue to pay attention to. So, pay attention, while there is still time.

To treat our own Mother Nature, we need to conserve her wellness, which means, we need to take every single measure that can promote her well-being. Every single measure that I am going to mention now, has utter significance in reducing the rate of global warming and slowly restoring a healthy environment around us.

Global warming is largely cause by greenhouse gas emissions. By taking actions that effect in reducing the greenhouse gas emission that you contribute in your personal life, you can take a real stand against global warming.

All you need to do is change your consumption habits and be efficient. Consume as less energy as possible, in any manner possible. Driving is the biggest ways people contribute to global warming. So, by minimizing driving, you can make a huge impact on Mother Earth. Here are some measures that you can take to minimize driving. Carpool to work with others. This not only reduces greenhouse gas emission, but also strengthens social bond. Use public transportation whenever possible, or ride a bike. If you own a car, then make sure that you maintain it regularly. This makes the car emit less greenhouse gas. Also, to reduce power consumption, replace the old incandescent light bulbs at home to compact fluorescent or LED bulbs. Especially LED bulbs are the most efficient so far, and can save a lot of power, also they are brighter than the old incandescent bulbs. This simple act of yours will not only reduce energy consumption but also it'll reduce your electricity bill.

These are the very simple few steps that you can take right away. You are not required to read thousands of books on global warming to make a real contribution in treating that global warming. It only takes the simple sense of responsibility. Do you feel that responsibility my friend? Do you? If you do, then start acting right now – at this very moment, and a few other humans around you will automatically learn from your actions and feel responsible enough to do their part as well. You cannot tell them to be responsible, you can only show them, how it is like to be responsible through your actions. These are not your legal responsibilities, but they are your human responsibilities.

However, the government will have to take certain legal steps on the matter of climate change on their part, without naively depending on the citizens.

Section 2. All street lights in a nation will be converted to solar powered LED lights by the national government.

Section 3. Vehicles running on fossil fuel, can be bought for personal usage, only if the customer gives consent to the city council that the vehicle will be used as a part of public transportation for two weeks every three months. A portion of the revenue will be offered to the owner of the vehicle, and the rest will be added to the city treasury. Also, any damage to the vehicle during its city service duration will be covered by the city council. Self-employed individuals and small business owners who require the vehicle as a part of their business, will be exempt from this service and can buy a vehicle with the option to choose not to let their vehicle used as public transport.

Our ancestors were naïve and ignorant on the matter of global warming, but we are better than them - and as such, we must act like we actually care about our future generations. So, I beg you my dear sibling – please act – don't stay silent and indifferent any more, to the agonies of Nature, because the agonies of Nature are getting worse and they'll destroy the very elements of wellness and joy in the life of your own children and grandchildren. Your indifference would only worsen the situation, so awake, arise and act – act not just for the rights of the humans but for the rights of Nature as well, because without the fundamental rights of wellness and peace restored in the heart of Mother Nature, humans will not have a home to rejoice their rights – their unity and their uniformity.

In The Valley of Liberty

There are two kinds of people in the world - those who make things happen and those who watch things happen. Now here is the ludicrous fact of the matter - everyone thinks that they are the ones who make things happen, and "others" are the ones who watch things happen, while in reality, they only delude themselves with such notion. Most of humanity are the watchers and only a handful are the "doers".

Now the question that we must ask is, what is a doer? And what kind of deed can be considered as a world-changing endeavor? Any act which you commit with the purest intension of benefiting another person, holds the power to change the world, for to change the world, we must first change human condition, and to change human condition on a global scale we must start local, by bringing a little change in the lives of the people around us.

Except for our pompous means of comfort, human condition is not much different from animal condition - we are tormented each day with animal like anxieties, insecurities and fears, and each torment makes us believe that perhaps having more comfort will change our condition, but it never does, rather, it only shoves us deeper into the abyss of psychological darkness.

However, like all elements of our perception, this darkness is a construct of our own mind, which can vanish quite instantly, once we begin to see the poison that truly ails us, and what ails us, is simply our devastatingly increasing desire for stimuli, and this desire manifests in varied manners, sometimes in the form of infidelity, sometimes consumerism, sometimes fundamentalism and sometimes political tyranny.

We can demolish all the chaos, loneliness, discrimination and wars of the world, once we simply get hold of our desires - and we can do so, not by force, but only by being aware of their harms. And by being aware, I am not saying to know about the harms, because having knowledge of the harms won't make any difference, unless you actually, genuinely, truly, feel the harms in your bones, like you feel the warmth of a hot cup of coffee if you hold it on your cheek.

Everything that I have mentioned in this constitution can only be brought to practice, if you truly realize the harms of prejudices, discriminations, selfishness and bigotry, in the deepest fathoms of your mind. If you do, then waste no more time, and rise right now - not tomorrow - not the day after tomorrow, but right now - rise and act with a genuine non-conflicting, priceless, ambitionless, humble and naïve desire to benefit the others. Be naïve, be humble, be human, that's all that is needed to heal this wounded world. Through your actions the world shall attain its real freedom.

Freedom is a complex term. And if you look a little deeper, you'll find out that, there never really was a question about having freedom. The humans, like all other animals, have always had freedom, that is, anybody could do anything, if they wanted. However, what the animals, and our primitive ancestors didn't have, was the brain capacity to comprehend the implications of their actions upon the lives of others.

Are you not free to think, speak or act, any way you like? You don't think, speak or act in a certain way, either because you have been conditioned by your environment in such a way, or because the law prohibits it and therefore you are afraid of it. Now, think, if you really wanted, you still can think, speak and do whatever you like. The results may vary, based on what's conceived to be normal in your environment, but your thought, speech and action are at all times free.

Now, all humans are given a guideline of individual freedom, and are conditioned to live within the guideline. And it is this sense of illusory obedience that defines the freedom of humans in a community, not the individual sense of responsibility. And that's where all the trouble begins. The world cannot be made humane and peaceful, unless the humans begin to redefine, recognize and realize their freedom based on their innate sense of responsibility towards their society, instead of being driven by obedience like racehorses.

Obedience may keep a society functioning, but a functioning society is not necessarily a humane society - even a bee hive is kept functioning, by the obedience-driven swarm of bees, but that doesn't make it a progressive and compassionate society of bees. The human society can be humane only if the humans act out of responsibility and not of obedience.

The humans are obedient, not observant, which is the main reason for all their problems of life, both as individuals and as a society. The obedient dies every day in the name of living, whereas the observant is the only one who knows the meaning of life. The meaning of life is not written in any book, old or new, for each life has the potential to manifest with unique meanings - however, in most cases, it doesn't, because the humans live as per the conditioning of their cultural environment. So, in order to rise as an original creature with original meaning in life, one must first accept the death of the identity imposed by one's culture.

Beyond culture, beyond tradition, beyond all dogmas and doctrines, there lies a beautiful valley full with real liberty and real harmony - in that valley, diversity is no cause for discrimination or hatred, rather it provides colors to the collective life of humanity as one family - in that valley, the best creed is to have no creed - the best path is to have no path - the best ideology is to have no ideology.

And remember, it is your personal journey, and as such it may not appeal to others, so don't mind the number of people who walk with you - as a matter of fact, if no one comes hearing your call, walk alone. In time, others will follow your footsteps, not necessarily in your lifetime.

Keep in mind, whatever you do, do it because that defines who you are, and not because you want to be popular among others. Action with expectation is a wastage of human potential. The world is so messed up because most humans simply tend to expect before they act, they believe before they know, they differentiate before they assimilate. And if this goes on, no amount of intellect or ideology will be able to sustain progress and harmony in a young species like ours. So, act beyond reward - think beyond dogmas - and feel beyond differences.

BIBLIOGRAPHY

Archer M., (2000), Being Human: The Problem of Agency. Cambridge University Press.

Archer M., (2003), Structure, Agency and the Internal Conversation. Cambridge University Press.

Adolphs R (2003) Cognitive neuroscience of human social behaviour. Nature Rev Neurosci 4: 165–178.

Adolphs R, Tranel D, Damasio AR (2003) Dissociable neural systems for recognizing emotions. Brain Cogn 52: 61–69.

Afton, A. D. (1985). Forced copulation as a reproductive strategy of male lesser scaup: A field test of some predictions. - Behaviour 92, p. 146-167.

Allison T, Puce A, McCarthy G. (2000) Social perception from visual cues: role of the STS region. Trends Cogn Sci 4: 267–278.

Andresen, Jensine, and Robert Forman, eds. Cognitive Models and Spiritual Maps. Bowling Green, Ohio: Imprint Academic, 2000.

Ashbrook, James, and Carol Albright. The Humanizing Brain: Where Religion and Neuroscience Meet. Cleveland, OH: Pilgrim Press, 1997.

Azari, Nina, Janpeter Nickel, Gilbert Wunderlich, Michael Niedeggen, Harald Hefter, Lutz Tellmann, Hans Herzog, Petra Stoerig, Dieter Birnbacher, and Rudiger Seitz. "Neural Correlates of Religious Experience." European Journal of Neuroscience 13, no. 8 (2001)

Agar, N. (2004). Liberal eugenics: In defence of human enhancement. London: Blackwell Publishing.

Alteheld, N., Roessler, G., Vobig, M., & Walter, R. (2004). The retina implant new approach to a visual prosthesis. Biomedizinische Technik, 49(4), 99–103.

Antal, A., Nitsche, M. A., Kincses, T. Z., Kruse, W., Hoffmann, K. P., & Paulus, W. (2004a). Facilitation of visuo-motor learning by transcranial direct current stimulation of the motor and extrastriate visual areas in humans. European Journal of Neuroscience, 19(10), 2888–2892.

Bhat Z, Kumar, S, Bhat H (2015) In vitro meat production. Challenges and benefits over conventional meat production. J Sci Food Agric 14: 241–248

Bernstein R. J., (1967), John Dewey. New York: Washington Square Press.

Bernstein R.J., (1971), Praxis and Action: Contemporary Philosophies of Human Activity. Philadelphia: University of Pennsylvania Press.

Bernstein R.J., (1976), The Restructuring Social and Political Thought.

Bernstein R.J., (1983), Beyond Relativism and Objectivism: Science, Hermeneutics, and Praxis. Philadelphia: University of Pennsylvania Press.

Bernstein R.J., (1986), Philosophical Profiles. Philadelphia: University of Pennsylvania Press.

Bernstein R.J., (1991), New Constellation. Cambridge: MIT Press.

Barash, D. P. (1977). Sociobiology of rape in mallards (Anas platyrhynchos): Responses of the mated male. - Science 197, p. 788-789.

Berger, J. (1986). Wild horses of the great basin: Social competition and population size. - The University of Chicago Press, Chicago.

Birkhead, T. R., Johnson, S. D. & Nettleship, D. N. (1985). Extra-pair matings and mate guarding in the common murre Uria aalge. - Anim. Behav. 33, p. 608-619.

Beauregard, Mario, and Vincent Paquette. "Neural Correlates of a Mystical Experience in Carmelite Nuns." Neuroscience Letters 405, no. 3 (2006)

Benson, Herbert. Timeless Healing: The Power and Biology of Belief. New York: Scribner, 1996

Bogen, J.E.(1995a), 'On the neurophysiology of consciousness: Part I. An overview', Consciousness and Cognition, 4.

Bogen, J.E. (1995b), 'On the neurophysiology of consciousness: Part II. Constraining the semantic problem', Consciousness and Cognition, 4.

Bremner, J. D., R. Soufer, et al. (2001). "Gender differences in cognitive and neural correlates of remembrance of emotional words." Psychopharmacol Bull 35 (3).

Brothers, L. (2002). The social brain: A project for integrating primate behavior and neurophysiology in a new domain. In J. T. Cacioppo et al. (Eds.), Foundations in neuroscience. Cambridge, MA: MIT Press.

Buss, D. D. (2003). Evolutionary Psychology: The New Science of Mind, 2nd ed. New York: Allyn & Bacon.

Buss, D. M. (1989). "Conflict between the sexes: Strategic interference and the evocation of anger and upset." J Pers Soc Psychol 56 (5).

Buss, D. M. (1995). "Psychological sex differences. Origins through sexual selection." Am Psychol 50 (3).

Buss, D. M. (2002). "Review: Human Mate Guarding." Neuro Endocrinol Lett 23 (Suppl 4).

Buss, D. M., and D. P. Schmitt (1993). "Sexual strategies theory: An evolutionary perspective on human mating." Psychol Rev 100 (2).

Blakemore SJ, Decety J (2001) From the perception of action to the understanding of intention. Nature Rev Neurosci 2: 561.

Bruce C, Desimone R, Gross CG (1981) Visual properties of neurons in a polysensory area in superior temporal sulcus of the macaque. J Neurophysiol 46: 369–384.

Buccino G, Vogt S, Ritzl A, Fink GR, Zilles K, Freund HJ, Rizzolatti G (2004) Neural circuits underlying imitation of hand actions: an event related fMRI study. Neuron 42: 323–34.

Colapietro V., (1988), "Human Agency: The Habits of Our Being."

Southern Journal of Philosophy, XXVI, 2, pp. 153-68.

Colapietro V., (1992), "Purpose, Power, and Agency." The Monist, 75, 4 (October) pp. 423-44.

Colapietro V., (2003), "Signs and their vicissitudes: Meanings in excess of consciousness and functionality." Logica, Dialogica, Ideologica, a cure di Susan Petrilli e Patrizia Calefato (Milano: Mimesis), pp. 221-36.

Colapietro V., (2004a), "C. S. Peirce's Reclamation of Teleology." Nature in American Philosophy, ed. Jean De Groot (Washington, D.C.: Catholic University Press of America), pp. 88-108.

Colapietro V., (2004b), "Portrait of a Historicist: An Alternative Reading of Peircean Semiotic." Semiotiche, 2/04 [maggio 2004], pp. 49-68.

Colapietro V., (2006), "Engaged Pluralism: Between Alterity and

Sociality." The Pragmatic Century: Conversations with Richard J. Bernstein (Albany, NY: SUNY Press), pp. 39-68.

Colapietro V., (2009), "Habit, Competence, and Purpose." Forthcoming in The Transactions of the Charles S. Peirce Society.

Calder AJ, Keane J, Manes F, Antoun N, Young AW (2000) Impaired recognition and experience of disgust following brain injury. Nature Neurosci 3: 1077–1078.

Carey DP, Perrett DI, Oram MW (1997) Recognizing, understanding and reproducing actions. In: Jeannerod M, Grafman J (eds) Handbook of neuropsychology. Vol. 11: Action and cognition. Elsevier, Amsterdam.

Carr L, Iacoboni M, Dubeau MC, Mazziotta JC, Lenzi GL (2003) Neural mechanisms of empathy in humans: a relay from neural systems for imitation to limbic areas. Proc Natl Acad Sci USA 100: 5497–5502.

Changeux JP, Ricoeur P (1998) La nature et la règle. Odile Jacob, Paris.

Cochin S, Barthelemy C, Roux S, Martineau J (1999) Observation and execution of movement: similarities demonstrated by quantified electroencephalograpy. Eur J Neurosci 11: 1839– 1842.

Chomsky Noam, (2017) Requiem for the American Dream

Chomsky Noam, (2016) Who Rules the World?

Chomsky Noam, (2010) How the World Works

Churchland, P.S. (1986), Neurophilosophy (Cambridge, MA: The MIT Press).

Churchland, P.S. & Ramachandran, V.S. (1993), 'Filling in: Why Dennett is wrong', in Dennett and His Critics: Demystifying Mind, ed. B. Dahlbom (Oxford: Blackwell Scientific Press).

Churchland, P.S., Ramachandran, V.S. & Sejnowski, T.J. (1994), 'A critique of pure vision', in Large- scale Neuronal Theories of the Brain, ed. C. Koch & J.L. Davis (Cambridge, MA: The MIT Press).

Crick, F. (1994), The Astonishing Hypothesis: The Scientific Search for the Soul (New York: Simon and Schuster).

Crick, F. (1996), 'Visual perception: rivalry and consciousness', Nature, 379.

Crick, F. & Koch, C. (1992), 'The problem of consciousness', Scientific American, 267.

Craig AD (2002) How do you feel? Interoception: the sense of the physiological condition of the body. Nature Rev Neurosci 3: 655–666.

Damasio, A (2003a) Looking for Spinoza. Harcourt Inc. Damasio A (2003b) Feeling of emotion and the self. Ann NY Acad Sci 1001: 253–261.

d'Aquili, Eugene. "Senses of Reality in Science and Religion." Zygon 17, no 4 (1982)

d'Aquili, Eugene. "The Biopsychological Determinants of Religious Ritual Behavior." Zygon 10, no. 1 (1975)

d'Aquili, Eugene. "The Myth-Ritual Complex: A Biogenetic Structural Analysis." Zygon 18, no. 3 (1983)

d'Aquili, Eugene, and Andrew Newberg. The Mystical Mind: Probing the Biology of Religious Experience. Minneapolis: Fortress Press, 1999.

Daly DD. 1958. Ictal affect. Am J Psychiatry.

Damasio, A. (1994) Descartes' Error: Emotion, Reason and the Human Brain. New York, Putnams.

Damasio, A. (1999) The Feeling of What Happens: Body, Emotion and the Making of Consciousness. London, Heinemann.

Darwin, C. (1859) On the Origin of Species by Means of Natural Selection. London, Murray.

Darwin, C. (1871) The Descent of Man and Selection in Relation to Sex. London, John Murray.

Darwin, C. (1872) The Expression of the Emotions in Man and Animals. London, John Murray; also published 1965, Chicago, University of Chicago Press.

Dawkins, M.S. (1987) Minding and mattering. In C. Blakemore and S. Greenfield (eds) Mindwaves. Oxford, Blackwell, 151-60.

Dawkins, R. (1976) The Selfish Gene. Oxford, Oxford University Press; a new edition, with additional material, was published in 1989.

Dawkins, R. (1986) The Blind Watchmaker. London, Longman.

Di Pellegrino G, Fadiga L, Fogassi L, Gallese V, Rizzolatti G (1992) Understanding motor events: A neurophysiological study. Exp Brain Res 91: 176–80.

Deikman, A.J. (2000) A functional approach to mysticism. Journal of Consciousness Studies 7(11-12), 75-91.

Delmonte, M.M. (1987) Personality and meditation. In M. West (ed.) The Psychology of Meditation. Oxford, Clarendon Press, 118-32.

Dennett, D.C. (1987) The Intentional Stance. Cambridge, MA, MIT Press.

Dennett, D.C. (1988) Quining qualia. In A.J. Marcel and E. Bisiach (eds)

Consciousness in Contemporary Science. Oxford, Oxford University Press, 42-77.

Dennett, D.C. (1991) Consciousness Explained. Boston, MA, and London, Little, Brown and Co.

Dennett, D.C. (1995a) Darwin's Dangerous Idea. London, Penguin.

Dennett, D.C. (1995b) The unimagined preposterousness of zombies. Journal of Consciousness Studies 2(4), 322-6.

Dennett, D.C. (1995c) Cog: steps towards consciousness in robots. In T. Metzinger (ed.) Conscious Experience. Thorverton, Devon, Imprint Academic, 471-87.

Dennett, D.C. (1995d) The path not taken. Behavioral and Brain Sciences 18, 252-3; commentary on N. Block, On a confusion about a function of consciousness. Behavioral and Brain Sciences 18, 227.

Dennett, D.C. (1996a) Facing backwards on the problem of consciousness. Journal of Consciousness Studies 3(1), 4-6.

Dennett, D.C. (1996b) Kinds of Minds: Towards an Understanding of Consciousness. London, Weidenfeld & Nicolson.

Dennett, D.C. (1997) An exchange with Daniel Dennett. In J. Searle (ed.) The Mystery of Consciousness. New York, New York Review of Books, 115-19.

Dennett, D.C. (1998) The myth of double transduction. In S.R. Hameroff, A.W. Kaszniak and A. C. Scott (eds) Toward a Science of Consciousness: The Second Tucson Discussions and Debates. Cambridge, MA, MIT Press, 97-107.

Dennett, D.C. (1998b) Brainchildren: Essays on Designing Minds. Cambridge, MA, MIT Press.

Dennett, D.C. (2001) The fantasy of first person science. Debate with D. Chalmers, Northwestern University, Evanston, IL, February 2001.

Dennett, D.C. (2003) Freedom Evolves. New York, Penguin.

Dennett, D.C. and Kinsbourne, M. (1992) Time and the observer: the where and when of consciousness in the brain. Behavioral and Brain Sciences 15, 183-247, including commentaries and authors' responses.

Dewey J., (1911 [1977]), "Epistemological Realism: The Alleged Ubiquity of the Knowledge Relation." Journal of Philosophy, VIII, 20 (September 28, 1911).

Dewhurst, Kenneth, and A. W. Beard. "Sudden Religious Conversions in Temporal Lobe Epilepsy." British Journal of Psychiatry 117 (1970)

Dewhurst K, Beard AW. Sudden religious conversions in temporal lobe epilepsy. 1970 Epilepsy Behav 2003

Devinsky O, Lai G. Spirituality and religion in epilepsy. Epilepsy Behav 2008.

Devinsky, O., Morrell, MJ, Vogt, BA. (1995) 'Contribution of anterior cingulate cortex to behavior', Brain, 118.

E. Horvitz, "One Hundred Year Study on Artificial Intelligence: Reflections and Framing," ed: Stanford University, 2014.

Eckhart Meister, Selected Writings

Egidi R., ed. (1999), "Von Wright and 'Dante's Dream': Stages in a Philosophical Pilgrim's Progress", in In Search of a New Humanism: the Philosophy of G.H. von Wright, ed. by R. Egidi, Kluwer, Dordrecht.

Fadiga L, Fogassi L, Pavesi G, Rizzolatti G (1995) Motor facilitation during action observation: a magnetic stimulation study. J Neurophysiol 73: 2608–2611.

Fogassi L, Gallese V, Fadiga L, Rizzolatti G (1998) Neurons responding to the sight of goal directed hand/arm actions in the parietal area PF (7b) of the macaque monkey. Soc Neurosci Abs 24:257.5.

Frith U, Frith CD (2003) Development and neurophysiology of mentalizing. Philos Trans R Soc Lond B Biol Sci 358: 459.

Farah, M.J. (1989), 'The neural basis of mental imagery', Trends in Neurosciences, 10.

Finlay BL, Darlington RB (1995) Linked regularities in the development and evolution of mammalian brains. Science 268.

Freud, S. "The Interpretation of Dreams", 1900

Freud, S. "Selected papers on hysteria and other psychoneuroses" Journal of Nervous and Mental Disease 1909.

Freud, S. "The Origin and Development of Psychoanalysis", 1910

Freud, S. "Psychopathology of everyday life", 1914

Freud, S. "Beyond the Pleasure Principle", 1920

Frith, C.D. & Dolan, R.J. (1997), 'Abnormal beliefs: Delusions and memory', Paper presented at the May, 1997, Harvard Conference on Memory and Belief.

Gay, Volney, ed. Neuroscience and Religion. Plymouth, UK: Lexington Books, 2009.

Gazzaniga, M. S. (1985). The social brain. New York: Basic Books.

Gazzaniga, M.S. (1993), 'Brain mechanisms and conscious experience', Ciba Foundation Symposium, 174.

Geschwind N. "Behavioural changes in temporal lobe epilepsy". Psychol Med. 1979.

Gellhorn, E., Kiely, W.F. "Mystical states of consciousness: neurophysiological and clinical aspects." J Nerv Ment Dis. 1972;154:399-405.

Gilbert SL, Dobyns WB, Lahn BT (2005) Genetic links between brain development and brain evolution. Nat Rev Genet 6.

Gray JA. The Psychology of Fear and Stress. 2nd ed. New York, NY: Cambridge University Press; 1988.

Gloor, P. (1992), 'Amygdala and temporal lobe epilepsy', in The Amygdala: Neurobiological Aspects of Emotion, Memory and Mental

Dysfunction, ed J.P. Aggleton (New York: Wiley-Liss).

Greenspan, S. I. and S. G. Shanker (2004). The first idea: How symbols, language, and intelligence evolved from our early primate ancestors to modern humans. Cambridge, MA: Da Capo Press.

Grady, D. (1993), 'The vision thing: Mainly in the brain', Discover, June.

Gallagher HL, Frith CD (2003) Functional imaging of 'theory of mind'. Trends Cogn Sci 7: 77.

Gallese V, Fogassi L, Fadiga L, Rizzolatti G (2002) Action representation and the inferior parietal lobule. In: Prinz W, Hommel B (eds) Attention & Performance XIX. Common mechanisms in perception and action. Oxford University Press, Oxford.

Gallese V, Keysers C, Rizzolatti G (2004) A unifying view of the basis of social cognition. Trends Cogn Sci 8: 396–403.

Gangitano M, Mottaghy FM, Pascual-Leone A (2001) Phase specific modulation of cortical motor output during movement observation. NeuroReport 12: 1489–1492.

Gangitano M, Mottaghy FM, Pascual-Leone A (2004) Modulation of premotor mirror neuron activity during observation of unpredictable grasping movements. Eur J Neurosci 20: 2193– 2202.

Goldman AI, Sripada CS (2004) Simulationist models of face-based emotion recognition. Cognition 94: 193–213.

Grèzes J, Costes N, Decety J (1998) Top-down effect of strategy on the perception of human biological motion: a PET investigation. Cogn Neuropsychol 15: 553–582.

Grèzes J, Armony JL, Rowe J, Passingham RE (2003) Activations related to "mirror" and "canonical" neurones in the human brain: an fMRI study. Neuroimage 18: 928–937.

Gross CG, Rocha-Miranda CE, Bender DB (1972) Visual properties of neurons in the inferotemporal cortex of the macaque. J Neurophysiol 35: 96–111.

Hari R, Forss N, Avikainen S, Kirveskari S, Salenius S, Rizzolatti G (1998) Activation of human primary motor cortex during action observation: a neuromagnetic study. Proc. Natl Acad Sci USA 95: 15061–15065.

Hall, Daniel, Keith Meador, and Harold Koenig. "Measuring Religiousness in Health Research: Review and Critique." Journal of Religion and Health 47, no. 2 (2008)

Harris, Sam, Jonas Kaplan, Ashley Curiel, Susan Bookheimer, Marco

Iacoboni, and Mark Cohen. "The Neural Correlates of Religious and Nonreligious Belief." PLoS One 4, no. 10 (October 1, 2009)

Halgren, E. (1992), 'Emotional neurophysiology of the amygdala within the context of human cognition', in The Amygdala: Neurobiological Aspects of Emotion, Memory and Mental Dysfunction, ed J.P. Aggleton (New York: Wiley-Liss).

Halligan PW, Fink GR, Marshal JC, Vallar G. 2003. Spatial cognition: evidence from visual neglect. Trends Cogn Sci.

Handbook of Emotions, Edited by Michael Lewis, Jeannette M. Haviland-Jones, and Lisa Feldman Barrett, The Guilford Press; 3rd edition (2010).

Haggard, P., Clark, S. and Kalogeras,]. (2002) Voluntary action and conscious awareness, Nature Neuroscience 5, 382-5. Haggard, P., Newman, C. and

Magno, E. (1999) On the perceived time of voluntary actions. British Journal of Psychology 90, 291-303.

Hameroff, S.R. and Penrose, R. (1996) Conscious events as orchestrated space-time selections. Journal of Consciousness Studies 3(1), 36-53; also reprinted in J. Shear (ed.) (1997) Explaining Consciousness-The Hard Problem. Cambridge, MA, MIT Press, 177-95.

Hardcastle, V.G. (2000) How to understand theN in NCC. InT. Metzinger (ed.) Neural Correlates of Consciousness. Cambridge, MA, MIT Press, 259-64.

Harding, D.E. (1961) On Having no Head: Zen and the Re-Discovery of the Obvious. London, Buddhist Society.

Hardy, A. (1979) The Spiritual Nature of Man: A Study of Contemporary Religious Experience. Oxford, Clarendon Press.

Hamad, S. (1990) The symbol grounding problem. Physica D 42, 335-46.

Hamad, S. (2001) No easy way out. The Sciences 41(2), 36-42.

Harre, R. and Gillett, G. (1994) The Discursive Mind. Thousand Oaks, CA, Sage.

Haugeland, J. (ed.) (1997) Mind Design II: Philosophy, Psychology, Artificial Intelligence. Cambridge, MA, MIT Press.

Hauser, M.D. (2000) Wild Minds: What Animals Really Think. New York, Henry Holt and Co.; London, Penguin.

Hearne, K. (1990) The Dream Machine. Northants, Aquarian.

Hebb, D.O. (1949) The Organization of Behavior. New York, Wiley.

Helmholtz, H.L.F. von (1856-67) Treatise on Physiological Optics.

Heyes, C.M. (1998) Theory of mind in nonhuman primates. Behavioral and Brain Sciences 21, 101-48; with commentaries.

Heyes, C.M. and Galef, B.G. (eds) (1996) Social Learning in Animals: The Roots of Culture. San Diego, CA, Academic Press.

Hilgard, E.R. (1986) Divided Consciousness: Multiple Controls in Human Thought and Action. New York, Wiley.

Hocquette JF (2016) Is in vitro meat the

solution for the future? Meat Science 120:

167–176

Hodgson, R. (1891) A case of double consciousness. Proceedings of the Society for Psychical Research 7, 221-58.

Hofstadter, D.R. (1979) Code!, Escher, Bach: An Eternal Golden Braid. London, Penguin.

Hofstadter, D.R. and Dennett, D.C. (eds) (1981) The Mind's I: Fantasies and Reflections on Self and Soul. London, Penguin.

Holland, J. (ed.) (2001) Ecstasy: The Complete Guide: A Comprehensive Look at the Risks and Benefits of MDMA. Rochester, VT, Park Street Press.

Holmes, D.S. (1987) The influence of meditation versus rest on physiological arousal. In M. West (ed.) The Psychology of Meditation. Oxford, Clarendon Press, 81-103.

Holt, J. (1999) Blindsight in debates about qualia. Journal of Consciousness Studies 6(5), 54-71.

Horgan, J. (1994), 'Can science explain consciousness?', Scientific American, 271.

Holloway RL (1996) Evolution of the human brain. In: Lock A, Peters CR (eds) Handbook of human symbolic evolution. Oxford University Press, Oxford

Iacoboni M, Woods RP, Brass M, Bekkering H, Mazziotta JC, Rizzolatti G (1999) Cortical mechanisms of human imitation. Science 286: 2526–2528.

Iacoboni M, Koski LM, Brass M, Bekkering H, Woods RP, Dubeau MC, Mazziotta JC, Rizzolatti G (2001) Reafferent copies of imitated actions in the right superior temporal cortex. Proc Natl Acad Sci USA 98: 13995–13999.

Jeannerod M (1988) The neural and behavioural organization of goal-directed movements. Clarendon Press, Oxford.

Johnson-Frey SH, Maloof FR, Newman-Norlund R, Farrer C, Inati S,

Grafton ST (2003) Actions or hand-objects interactions? Human inferior frontal cortex and action observation. Neuron 39: 1053–1058.

Jackson, F. (1982) Epiphenomenal qualia. Philosophical Quarterly 32, 127-36.

James, W. (1890) The Principles of Psychology (2 volumes). London, Macmillan.

James, W. (1902) The Varieties of Religious Experience: A Study in Human Nature. New York and London, Longmans, Green and Co.

Jansen, K. (2001) Ketamine: Dreams and Realities. Sarasota, FL, Multidisciplinary Association for Psychedelic Studies.

Jay, M. (ed.) (1999) Artificial Paradises: A Drugs Reader. London, Penguin.

Jaynes, J. (1976) The Origin of Consciousness in the Breakdown of the Bicameral Mind. New York, Houghton Mifflin.

Johnson, M.K. and Raye, C.L. (1981) Reality monitoring. Psychological Review 88, 67-85.

Kadim I, Mahgoub O, Baqir S et al. (2015) Cultured meat from muscle stem cells: a review of challenges and prospects. J Integr Agr 14: 222–233

Koski L, Iacoboni M, Dubeau MC, Woods RP, Mazziotta JC (2003) Modulation of cortical activity during different imitative behaviors. J Neurophysiol 89: 460–471.

Krolak-Salmon P, Henaff MA, Isnard J, Tallon-Baudry C, Guenot M, Vighetto A, Bertrand O, Mauguiere F (2003) An attention modulated response to disgust in human ventral anterior insula. Ann Neurol 53: 446–453.

Kandel, E. R. In Search of Memory: The Emergence of a New Science of

Mind, W. W. Norton & Company (2007).

Kandel E. R. Schwartz JH, Jessel TM. Principles of neural sciences. New York; McGraw Hill, 2000.

Kanizsa, G. (1979), Organization In Vision (New York: Praeger).

Kaloupek DG, Scott JR, Khatami V. Assessment of coping strategies associated with syncope in blood donors. J Psychosom Res. 1985;29:207-214.

Kanwisher, N. (2001) Neural events and perceptual awareness. Cognition 79, 89-113; also reprinted inS. Dehaene (ed.) The Cognitive Neuroscience of Consciousness. Cambridge, MA, MIT Press, 89-113.

Kapleau, Roshi P. (1980) The Three Pillars of Zen: Teaching, Practice, and Enlightenment (revised edn). New York, Doubleday.

Karn, K. and Hayhoe, M. (2000) Memory representations guide targeting eye movements in a natural task. Visual Cognition 7, 673-703.

Kasamatsu, A. and Hirai, T. (1966) An electroencephalographic study on the Zen meditation (zazen). Folia Psychiatrica et Neurologica Japonica 20, 315-36.

Kaiserman-Abramof, I. R., Graybiel, A. M., & Nauta, W. J. (1980). The thalamic projection to cortical area 17 in a congenitally anophthalmic mouse strain. Neuroscience, 5, 41–52.

Kanold, P. O., Kara, P., Reid, R. C., & Shatz, C. J. (2003). Role of subplate neurons in functional maturation of visual cortical columns. Science, 301, 521–525.

Kennedy, H., & Dehay, C. (1988). Functional implications of the anatomical organization of the callosal projections of visual areas V1 and V2 in the macaque monkey. Behav. Brain Res., 29, 225–236.

Kennedy, H., & Dehay, C. (1993). Cortical specifi cation of mice and men. Cereb. Cortex, 3, 171–186.

Kentridge, R.W. and Heywood, C.A. (1999) The status of blindsight. Journal of Consciousness Studies 6(5), 3-11.

Kihlstrom, J.F. (1996) Perception without awareness of what is perceived, learning without awareness of what is learned. In M. Velmans (ed.) The Science of Consciousness. London, Routledge, 23-46.

Kluver, H. (1926) Mescal visions and eidetic vision. American Journal of Psychology 37, 502-15.

Kollerstrom, N. (1999) The path of Halley's comet, and Newton's late apprehension of the law of gravity. Annals of Science 56, 331-56.

Kosslyn, S.M. (1980) Image and Mind. Cambridge, MA, Harvard University Press.

Kosslyn, S.M. (1988) Aspects of a cognitive neuroscience of mental imagery. Science 240, 1621-6.

Kinsbourne, M. (1995), 'The intralaminar thalamic nucleii', Consciousness and Cognition, 4.

Kjaer, Troels, Camilla Bertelsen, Paola Piccini, David Brooks, Jorgen Alving, and Hans Lou. "Increased Dopamine Tone during Meditation- Induced Change of Consciousness." Cognitive Brain Research 13, no. 2 (April 2002)

Kölmel HW. 1985. Complex visual hallucinations in the hemianopic field. J Neurol Neurosurg Psychiatry.

Koenig, Harold. "Research on Religion, Spirituality, and Mental Health: A Review." Canadian Journal of Psychiatry 54, no. 5 (May 2009)

Koenig, Harold, ed. Handbook of Religion and Mental Health. San Diego, CA: Academic Press, 1998

Kraepelin E. Psychiatry: A Textbook for Students and Physicians. New York, NY: Science History Publications; 1990.

Lauglin, Charles, John McManus, and Eugene d'Aquili. Brain, Symbol, and Experience. 2nd ed. New York: Columbia University Press, 1992

Lakoff, G. and M. Johnson (1999). Philosophy in the flesh. Basic Books: New York.

LeDoux, J. E. (1996). The emotional brain. New York: Simon & Schuster.

LeDoux, J.E. (1992), 'Emotion and the amygdala', in The Amygdala: Neurobiological Aspects of Emo- tion, Memory and Mental Dysfunction, ed J.P. Aggleton (New York: Wiley-Liss).

Levin, D.T. and Simons, D.J. (1997) Failure to detect changes to attended objects in motion pictures. Psychonomic Bulletin and Review 4, 501-6.

Levine,J. (1983) Materialism and qualia: the explanatory gap. Pacific Philosophical Quarterly 64, 354-61.

Levine,J. (2001) Purple Haze: The Puzzle of Consciousness. New York, Oxford University Press. Levine, S. (1979) A Gradual Awakening. New York, Doubleday.

Levinson, B.W. (1965) States of awareness during general anaesthesia. British Journal of Anaesthesia 37, 544-6.

Lewicki, P., Czyzewska, M. and Hoffman, H. (1987) Unconscious acquisition of complex procedural knowledge. Journal of Experimental Psychology: Learning, Memory and Cognition 13, 523-30.

Lewicki, P., Hill, T. and Bizot, E. (1988) Acquisition of procedural knowledge about a pattern of stimuli that cannot be articulated. Cognitive Psychology 20, 24-37.

Lewicki, P., Hill, T. and Czyzewska, M. (1992) Nonconscious acquisition of information. American Psychologist 47, 796-801.

Manthey S, Schubotz RI, von Cramon DY (2003). Premotor cortex in observing erroneous action: an fMRI study. Brain Res Cogn Brain Res 15: 296–307.

M. Colombo, "Why build a virtual brain? Large-scale neural simulations as jump start for cognitive computing," Journal of Experimental and Theoretical Artificial Intelligence, vol. 29, pp. 361-370, 2017.

Mesulam MM, Mufson EJ (1982) Insula of the old world monkey. III: Efferent cortical output and comments on function. J Comp Neurol 212: 38–52.

Naskar, Abhijit. "What is Mind?", 2016

Naskar, Abhijit. "In Search of Divinity: Journey to The Kingdom of Conscience", 2016

Naskar, Abhijit. "Love, God & Neurons: Memoir of A Scientist who found himself by getting lost", 2016

Naskar, Abhijit. "Neurons of Jesus: Mind of A Teacher, Spouse & Thinker", 2017

Naskar, Abhijit. "Rowdy Buddha: The First Sapiens", 2017

Naskar, Abhijit. "The Education Decree", 2017

Naskar, Abhijit. "Principia Humanitas", 2017

Naskar, Abhijit. "We Are All Black: A Treatise on Racism", 2017

Naskar, Abhijit. "Wise Mating: A Treatise on Monogamy", 2017

Naskar, Abhijit. "Illusion of Religion: A Treatise on Religious Fundamentalism", 2017

Naskar, Abhijit. "I Am The Thread: My Mission", 2017

Naskar, Abhijit. "Morality Absolute", 2017

Newberg, Andrew, and Jeremy Iversen. "The Neural Basis of the Complex Mental Task of Meditation: Neurotransmitter and Neurochemical Considerations." Medical Hypotheses 61, no. 2 (2003).

Newberg, Andrew. "How God Changes Your Brain: An Introduction to Jewish Neurotheology", CCAR Journal: The Reform Jewish Quarterly, Winter 2016.

Newberg, Andrew, and Stephanie Newberg. "A Neuropsychological Perspective on Spiritual Development." In Handbook of Spiritual Development in Childhood and Adolescence, edited by Eugene Roehlkepartain, Pamela King, Linda Wagener, and Peter Benson. London: Sage Publications, Inc., 2005

Newberg, Andrew. "The Neurotheology Link An Intersection Between Spirituality and Health", Alternative and Complimentary Therapies, Vol 21 No 1, February 2015.

Newberg, Andrew, Nancy Wintering, Dharma Khalsa, Hannah Roggenkamp, and Mark Waldman. "Meditation Effects on Cognitive Function and Cerebral Blood Flow in Subjects with Memory Loss: A Preliminary Study." Journal of Alzheimer's Disease 20, no. 2 (2010)

Nash, M. (1995), 'Glimpses of the mind', Time.

Nesse RM. Proximate and evolutionary studies of anxiety, stress and depression: synergy at the interface. Neurosci Biobehav Rev. 1999;23:895-903.

Nishitani N, Hari R (2000) Temporal dynamics of cortical representation for action. Proc Natl Acad Sci USA 97: 913–918.

Nishitani N, Hari R (2002) Viewing lip forms: cortical dynamics. Neuron 36: 1211–1220.

O'Hara, K. and Scutt, T. (1996) There is no hard problem of consciousness. Journal of Consciousness Studies 3(4), 290-302, reprinted in J. Shear (ed.) (1997) Explaining Consciousness. Cambridge, MA, MIT Press, 69-82.

O'Regan, J.K. (1992) Solving the "real" mysteries of visual perception: the world as an outside memory. Canadian Journal of Psychology 46, 461-88.

O'Regan, J.K. and Noe, A. (2001) A sensorimotor account of vision and visual consciousness. Behavioral and Brain Sciences 24(5), 883-917.

O'Regan, J.K., Rensink, R.A. and Clark,].]. (1999) Change-blindness as a result of "mudsplashes." Nature 398, 34.

Ornstein, R.E. (1977) The Psychology of Consciousness (2nd edn). New York, Harcourt.

Ornstein, R.E. (1986) The Psychology of Consciousness (3rd edn). New York, Pehguin.

Ornstein, R.E. (1992) The Evolution of Consciousness. New York, Touchstone.

Penfield W, Faulk ME (1955) The insula: further observations on its function. Brain 78: 445– 470.

Penrose, R. (1994), Shadows of the Mind (Oxford: Oxford University Press).

Penrose, R. (1989), The Emperor's New Mind: Concerning Computers, Minds and The Laws of Physics (Oxford: Oxford University Press).

Persinger, "'I would kill in God's name' role of sex, weekly church attendance, report of a religious experience and limbic lability" Perceptual and Motor Skills 1997.

Persinger "Experimental simulation of the God experience" Neurotheology 2003.

Persinger, M. A. (1993b). Personality changes following brain injury as a grief response to the loss of sense of self: Phenomenological themes as indices of local lability and neurocognitive restructuring as psycho- therapy. Psychological Reports, 72

Persinger, Corradini, Clement, Keaney, et al "Neurotheology and its convergence with neuroquantology" NeuroQuantology 2010.

Persinger, Koren and St-Pierre "The electromagnetic induction of mystical and altered states within the laboratory" Journal of Consciousness Exploration and Research 2010.

Persinger "Case report: A prototypical spontaneous 'sensed presence' of a sentient being and concomitant electroencephalographic activity in the clinical laboratory" Neurocase 2008.

Persinger and Saroka "Potential production of Hughlings Jackson's "parasitic consciousness" by physiologically-patterned weak transcerebral magnetic fields: QEEG and source localization" Epilepsy & Behavior 28 (2013).

Persinger. "The neuropsychiatry of paranormal experiences". J Neuropsychiatry Clin Neurosci 2001.

Persinger. "Neuropsychological bases of god beliefs", New York: Praeger, 1987

Persinger. "Temporal lobe epileptic signs and correlative behaviors displayed by normal populations", Journal of General Psychology, 1986

Persinger "Experimental Facilitation of the Sensed Presence: Possible Intercalation between the Hemispheres Induced by Complex Magnetic Fields" Journal of Nervous and Mental Disease 2002.

Palmer J. 1978. The out-of-body experience: a psychological theory. Parapsychol Rev.

Page AC. Blood-injury phobia. Clinical Psychology Review. 1994;14:443-461.

Perry BD, Pollard R. Homeostasis, stress, trauma, and adaptation. A neurodevelopmental view of childhood trauma. Child Adolesc Psychiatr Clin N Am. 1998;7:33.

Paré, D. & Llinás, R. (1995), 'Conscious and preconscious processes as seen from the standpoint of sleep-waking cycle neurophysiology', Neuropsychologia, 33.

P. S. de Laplace. Essai Philosophique sur les Probabilites [1814], in Academy des Sciences, Oeuvres Complotes de Laplace, Vol. 7, Gauthier-Villars, Paris (1886).

Perrett DI, Harries MH, Bevan R, Thomas S, Benson PJ, Mistlin AJ, Chitty AJ, Hietanen JK, Ortega JE (1989) Frameworks of analysis for the neural representation of animate objects and actions. J Exp Bio 146: 87–113.

Phillips ML, Young AW, Senior C, Brammer M, Andrew C, Calder AJ, Bullmore ET, Perrett DI, Rowland D, Williams SC, Gray JA, David AS (1997) A specific neural substrate for perceiving facial expressions of disgust. Nature 389: 495–498.

Phillips ML, Young AW, Scott SK, Calder AJ, Andrew C, Giampietro V, Williams SC, Bullmore ET, Brammer M, Gray JA (1998) Neural responses to facial and vocal expressions of fear and disgust. Proc R Soc Lond B Biol Sci 265: 1809–1817.

Puce A, Perrett D (2003) Electrophysiological and brain imaging of biological motion. Philosoph Trans Royal Soc Lond, Series B, 358: 435–445.

Ramachandran VS. Behavioral and magnetoencephalographic correlates of plasticity in the adult human brain. Proc Natl Acad Sci USA 1993; 90: 10413–20.

Ramachandran VS. Phantom limbs, neglect syndromes, repressed memories, and Freudian psychology. Int Rev Neurobiol 1994; 37: 291–333.

Ramachandran VS. Plasticity and functional recovery in neurology. Clin Med 2005; 5: 368–73.

Ramachandran VS, Hirstein W. The perception of phantom limbs. The D. O. Hebb lecture. Brain 1998; 121: 1603–30.

Ramachandran VS, McGeoch PD, Williams L, Arcilla G. Rapid relief of thalamic pain syndrome induced by vestibular caloric stimulation. Neurocase 2007; 13: 185–8.

Ramachandran VS, Rogers-Ramachandran D, Cobb S. Touching the phantom limb. Nature 1995; 377: 489–90.

Ramachandran VS, Rogers-Ramachandran D. Phantom limbs and neural plasticity. Arch Neurol 2000; 57: 317–20.

Ramachandran VS, Rogers-Ramachandran D. It's all done with mirrors. Sci Am Mind 2007; 18: 16–9.

Ramachandran VS, Rogers-Ramachandran D. Sensations referred to a patient's phantom arm from another subjects intact arm: perceptual correlates of mirror neurons. Med Hypotheses 2008; 70: 1233–4.

Ramachandran VS, Rogers-Ramachandran D, Stewart M. Perceptual correlates of massive cortical reorganization. Science 1992; 258: 1159–60.

Rizzolatti G, Craighero L (2004) The mirror-neuron system. Annu Rev Neurosci 27: 169–192.

Rizzolatti G, Scandolara C, Matelli M, Gentilucci M (1981) Afferent properties of periarcuate neurons in macaque monkeys. I. Somatosensory responses. Behav Brain Res 2: 125–146.

Rizzolatti G, Fadiga L, Matelli M, Bettinardi V, Paulesu E, Perani D, Fazio F (1996) Localization of grasp representation in humans by PET: 1.

Observation versus execution. Exp Brain Res 111: 246–252.

Rizzolatti G, Fogassi L, Gallese V (2001) Neurophysiological mechanisms underlying the understanding and imitation of action. Nature Rev Neurosci 2:661–670.

Rock I, Victor J. Vision and touch: an experimentally created conflict between the two senses. Science 1964; 143: 594–6.

Rose´n B, Lundborg G. Training with a mirror in rehabilitation of the hand. Scand J Plast Reconstr Surg Hand Surg 2005; 39: 104–8.

Royet JP, Plailly J, Delon-Martin C, Kareken DA, Segebarth C (2003) fMRI of emotional responses to odors: influence of hedonic valence and judgment, handedness, and gender. Neuroimage 20: 713–728.

Rozin R Haidt J and McCauley CR (2000) Disgust. In: Lewis M, Haviland-

Jones JM (eds) Handbook of Emotion. 2nd Edition. Guilford Press, New York, pp 637–653.

Saxe R, Carey S, Kanwisher N (2004) Understanding other minds: linking developmental psychology and functional neuroimaging. Annu Rev Psychol 55: 87–124.

S. J. Russell and P. Norvig, Artificial intelligence: a modern approach (3rd edition): Prentice Hall, 2009.

Schienle A, Stark R, Walter B, Blecker C, Ott U, Kirsch P, Sammer G, Vaitl D (2002) The insula is not specifically involved in disgust processing: an fMRI study. Neuroreport 13: 2023–2026.

Showers MJC, Lauer EW (1961) Somatovisceral motor patterns in the insula. J Comp Neurol 117: 107–115.

Singer T, Seymour B, O'Doherty J, Kaube H, Dolan RJ, Frith CD (2004) Empathy for pain involves the affective but not the sensory components of pain. Science 303: 1157–1162.

Small DM, Gregory MD, Mak YE, Gitelman D, Mesulam MM, Parrish T (2003) Dissociation of neural representation of intensity and affective valuation in human gustation Neuron 39: 701–711.

Smith A (1759) The theory of moral sentiments (ed. 1976). Clarendon Press, Oxford.

Sprengelmeyer R, Rausch M, Eysel UT, Przuntek H (1998) Neural structures associated with recognition of facial expressions of basic emotions Proc R Soc Lond B Biol Sci 265: 1927–1931.

Strafella AP, Paus T (2000) Modulation of cortical excitability during action observation: a transcranial magnetic stimulation study. NeuroReport 11: 2289–2292.

Simonsen R (2015) Eating for the future: veganism and the challenge of in vitro meat. In: Stapleton P, Byers A (Hg). Biopolitics and utopia. Palgrave Macmillan, New York (2015), S 167–190

Tanaka K (1996) Inferotemporal cortex and object vision. Ann Rev Neurosci. 19: 109–140.

T. R. Society, "Machine learning: the power and promise of computers that learn by example," ed. The Royal Society, 2017.

Tomasello M, Call J (1997) Primate cognition. Oxford University Press, Oxford.

Tremblay C, Robert M, Pascual-Leone A, Lepore F, Nguyen DK, Carmant L, Bouthillier A, Theoret H (2004) Action observation and execution: intracranial recordings in a human subject. Neurology. 63: 937–938.

Umilta MA, Kohler E, Gallese V, Fogassi L, Fadiga L, Keysers C, Rizzolatti G (2001) "I know what you are doing": a neurophysiological study. Neuron 32: 91–101.

Von Wright G.H., (1963), Norm and Action. A Logical Inquiry, Routledge & Kegan Paul, London.

Von Wright G.H., (1976), "Determinism and the Study of Man", in Essays on Explanation and Understanding, ed. by J. Manninen and R. Tuomela, Reidel, Dordrecht.

Von Wright G.H., (1977), "What is Humanism?", The Lindlay Lecture, University of Arkansas, Lawrence, Kansas.

Von Wright G.H., (1979), "Humanism and the Humanities", in Philosophy and Grammar, ed. by S. Kanger and S. Öhman, Reidel, Dordrecht, pp. 1-16. Reprinted in von Wright (1993).

Von Wright G.H., (1980), Freedom and Determination, North-Holland Publishing Co., Amsterdam.

Von Wright G.H., (1985), Of Human Freedom, The Tanner Lectures on Human Values,

Vol. VI, ed. by S. M. McMurrin, University of Utah Press, Salt Lake City, pp. 107-70. Reprinted in von Wright (1998).

Von Wright G.H., (1993), The Tree of Knowledge and Other Essays, Brill, Leiden.

Von Wright G.H., (1997), "Progress: Fact and Fiction", in The Idea of Progress, ed. by A. Burgen et al., W. de Gruyter, Berlin, pp. 1-18.

Von Wright G.H., (1998), In the Shadow of Descartes: Essays in the Philosophy of Mind, Kluwer, Dordrecht.

Visalberghi E, Fragaszy D. (2002). Do monkeys ape? Ten years after. In: Dautenhahn K, Nehaniv C (eds) Imitation in animals and artifacts. MIT Press, Boston. Pp. 471–500

Weele C, Driessen C. (2016) In vitro meat is a chance to rethink. In: Stephens N, Kramer C, Denfeld Z, Strand R (Hg). What is in vitro meat? Food Phreaking Issue 02: 57–59

Wicker B, Keysers C, Plailly J, Royet JP, Gallese V, Rizzolatti G (2003) Both of us disgusted in my insula: the common neural basis of seeing and feeling disgust. Neuron 40: 655–664.

Yokochi H, Tanaka M, Kumashiro M, Iriki A (2003) Inferior parietal somatosensory neurons coding face-hand coordination in Japanese macaques. Somatosens Mot Res 20 : 115–125.

Zald DH, Pardo JV (2000) Functional neuroimaging of the olfactory system in humans. Int J Psychophysiol 36: 165–181.

Zald DH, Donndelinger MJ, Pardo JV (1998) Elucidating dynamic brain interactions with across-subjects correlational analyses of positron emission tomographic data: the functional connectivity of the amygdala and orbitofrontal cortex during olfactory tasks. J Cereb Blood Flow Metab 18: 896–905.

www.ingramcontent.com/pod-product-compliance
Lightning Source LLC
Chambersburg PA
CBHW051443250726
48655CB00001B/218